TIMES OF
Refreshing

Inspiration, Prayers, and God's Word for Each Day

BOOKS BY DR. JOE IBOJIE

Bible-Based Dictionary
of Prophetic Symbols for Every Christian

The Watchman

Dreams and Visions Volume 1
International Best Seller

Dreams and Visions Volume 2

The Justice of God: Victory in Everyday Living

How to Live the Supernatural Life in the Here and Now
International Best Seller

Illustrated Bible-Based Dictionary of Dream Symbols
International Best Seller

The Final Frontiers—Countdown to the Final Showdown

Destined for the Top
New

Times of Refreshing
New

AVAILABLE FROM CROSS HOUSE BOOKS

TIMES OF
Refreshing

Inspiration, Prayers, and God's Word for Each Day

Dr. Joe Ibojie &
Pastor Cynthia Ibojie

CROSS HOUSE BOOKS
Christian Book Publishers
245 Midstocket Road
Aberdeen
AB15 5PH, UK

"The entrance of Your Word brings light."

ISBN: 978-0-9564008-6-4

For Worldwide Distribution, Printed in U.S.A.

1 2 3 4 5 6 7 / 16 15 14 13 12

To order products by Dr. Joe Ibojie & other Cross House Books, contact sales@crosshousebooks.co.uk.

Other correspondence: info@crosshousebooks.co.uk.

Visit www.crosshousebooks.co.uk.

Endorsement

THIS book takes you beyond teaching to a devotional journey. You will discover the wonder and glory of the nature of God in each meditation. These bite-size teachings will help you balance your daily Bible study and increase your passion for God. Dr. Joe Ibojie and Pastor Cynthia Ibojie have used daily inspirations to build hands-on opportunities for Holy Spirit encounters for you.

Dr. Sharon Stone
President and founder, Christian International Europe
Birmingham, UK
cieurope@aol.co.uk

Introduction

E ACH message in this book was birthed out of our quiet time with the Lord. We allowed each message a time of maturation and to be quintessentially breathed upon and brooded on by the Holy Spirit Himself. Since working on this project, we have come to see the essence of one of Apostle Peter's statements as it bears relevance to our daily living:

> For no prophecy ever originated because some man willed it [to do so—it never came by human impulse], but men spoke from God who were borne along (moved and impelled) by the Holy Spirit (2 Peter 1:21 AMP).

This passage from Second Peter is also succinctly put in the Message Bible rendition:

> The main thing to keep in mind here is that no prophecy of Scripture is a matter of private opinion. And why? Because it's not something concocted in the human heart. Prophecy resulted when the Holy Spirit prompted men and women to speak God's Word.

We testify to this truth and confess that perhaps we should claim no ownership of this work but only admit the work of the Holy Spirit who has indeed graciously *"moved and impelled"* us over these several years. Many in our local congregation have found inspiration and encouragement from these messages, and we pray they will inspire you to greater height in God.

This work is not meant to be a theological treatise nor preaching on doctrinal principles but rather they are messages of inspiration and of hopes for troubled times. As the Bible says, *"I want you to trust Me in your times of troubles, so I can rescue you, and you can give Me glory"* (Ps. 50:14-15 Living Bible).

These messages are written to give encouragement and strength to you and so help to build up trust in God in good times and on the day that is evil.

Prayers for the New Year

"I [the Lord] *will return to Jerusalem with mercy, and there my house will be rebuilt. And the measuring line will be stretched out over Jerusalem,"* declares the Lord Almighty (Zechariah 1:16 and also see 2:1-5).

OUR local church and I observe a collective fast at the end of each year to prepare us for the coming year. Our end-of-the-year fast is from December 27 to 31, but you can pray and fast any time during the year. Often we use the following passages as the focus:

- Isaiah 58:6 (KJV) - *break the bond of wickedness*
- Joshua 3:5 - *consecration for promotion/advancement*
- Judges 11:23-24 - *we will possess what the Lord has given us*
- 2 Kings 4:7 - *market place dominance; sell your oil, pay off debts and live in surplus*

Slowly but surely the hour draws nearer, the time for your manifestation has come. Just as Zechariah saw an angel with a measuring line on a mission to ascertain whether the foundation of Jerusalem is firm and big enough for expected blessings, so I see the Lord strengthening your stakes for the blessings He has for you in the coming year.

**Are you expecting God's best for the New Year?
For this week? For today?**

Earth Rulers—Kingdom Agents

*Then God blessed them, and God said to them, "Be fruitful and multiply; fill the earth and subdue it; **have dominion** over the fish of the sea, over the birds of the air, and over every living thing that moves on the earth"* (Genesis 1:28 NKJV).

GOD has delegated to all of His children, all believers in Jesus Christ, all authority as His Kingdom agents on earth. He said, *"be fruitful and multiply...subdue...have dominion."* As earth rulers, let us exercise our dominion power and realize that prayer time is power time! As God's Kingdom agents, we wear His armor. One of the essential weapons we carry is the Word of God.

The Word of God is in our mouth and His words are power-ful because they are spirits and they are life. Use God's words today as they surely are spirit and life to all who believe. For this reason, humankind occupies a special place in God's creation order, *"what is mankind that you* [God] *are mindful of them, human beings that you care for them? "You have made them a little lower than the angels and crowned them with glory and honor"* (Psalm 8:4-5 NIV).

May you always remain fruitful as you exercise your dominion authority as an earth ruler.

Do you look, act, and feel as if you are crowned with
God's glory and honor? That you have dominion
over your surroundings?

Rehoboth

He moved on from there and dug another well, and no one quarrelled over it. He named it Rehoboth, saying, "Now the LORD has given us room and we will flourish in the land"
(Genesis 26:22 NIV).

As a child of God, each day has a lesson to teach each child of God. Each one of us should know what God is teaching us by the thing He doing through the circumstances He allows to confront us.

In the Book of Genesis, we know that God in His omnipotence could have stopped the harassment of Isaac and his men from the hands of the Philistines, but in His infinite wisdom he did not! Instead, He allowed them to go through the hardship and endure ridicule in order to bring them to the place where He made room for them.

We should never give up on our dreams and never give up praying until the answers come. If God opens a door for you, no one can close it. Don't waste time and fail to learn the lesson of the experience that may come across your path in life. Learn to gain the wisdom of the time, because He makes everything beautiful in its time. So when He says, *"Rehoboth,"* be encouraged to walk into your inheritance unhindered.

Do you know when it is time to move on—to move into the room God made for you?

Reading the Bible in a Year: Genesis 6-8 & Matthew 3.

One Thing Is Needful

One thing I ask from the LORD, this only do I seek: that I may dwell in the house of the LORD all the days of my life, to gaze on the beauty of the LORD and to seek him in his temple. For in the day of trouble he will keep me safe in his dwelling; he will hide me in the shelter of his sacred tent and set me high upon a rock (Psalm 27:4-5).

Of all the things that are important in our lives, none is as important as seeking the face of God. In His presence, there is joy forevermore; therefore joy unlimited awaits us if we seek His presence. Where would anyone rather be other than His presence?

Remember the story of Martha and Mary, when they had the uncommon privilege of hosting Jesus? One chose to stay at His feet and the other chose to focus mainly on busyness, making provision to serve Him. Though both are right, beneath the surface, one is weightier. That is why Jesus made this remarkable statement that only one thing was needful, *"Martha, Martha," the Lord answered, "you are worried and upset about many things, but few things are needed—or indeed only one. Mary has chosen what is better, and it will not be taken away from her"* (Luke 10:40-42). The one who chose to stay at His feet had chosen the needful thing!

From today on, seek His face at all times, and you will always choose the needful thing.

Are you too busy to seek the needful thing?

Don't Be Weary in Doing Well

*Let us not become weary in doing good, for at the proper time
we will reap a harvest if we do not give up* (Galatians 6:9).

SOMETIMES we do not get the results we expect. Bad things may happen to good people and good things may happen to bad people—but this we can sure of, God sees everything and He will reward everyone according to the deeds each person has done.

The Scriptures say not to become weary in well-doing, for in due season you will surely reap your reward if you faint not! Love never fails, and goodness will always pay off. Others may take you for granted, but God sees everything. Even the good you have done in secret, will speak out for you some day. Your labor of love will not go unrewarded!

Are you weary? Have you given up?
Pray on Galatians 6:9.

Those Who Can Do Exploits

*Who, then, are **those who fear the LORD**? He will instruct them in the ways they should choose. They will spend their days in **prosperity**, and their descendants will **inherit the land**. The LORD confides in those who fear him; he **makes his covenant known** to them* (Psalm 25:12-14).

THE Bible describes those who are able to do great exploits as they who know their God. They are the ones who will be made strong. God knows everyone and everything, but it is only those who know Him who will be made strong to do exploits for Him (see Dan. 11:32). Knowing God comes by revelation and His revelation comes by reverent fear of God—as God confides in those who fear Him.

Since exploits belong to those who know their God, then revelation is pivotal. This is the compelling story of two kings, one with access to revelation and the other only operated on information: *"Now the king of Aram was at war with Israel. After conferring with his officers, he said, "I will set up my camp in such and such a place." The man of God sent word to the king of Israel: "Beware of passing that place, because the Arameans are going down there." So the king of Israel checked on the place indicated by the man of God. Time and again Elisha warned the king, so that he was on his guard in such places. This enraged the king of Aram. He summoned his officers and demanded of them, "Tell me! Which of us is on the side of the king of Israel?" "None of us, my lord the king," said one of his officers, "but Elisha, the prophet who is in Israel, tells the king of Israel the very words you speak in your bedroom"* (2 Kings 6:8-12). By revelation given to him by the prophet Elisha, the king of Israel gained advantage over the king of Aram and did great exploits.

Be ahead of the devil and his agents, get some revelation!

Are you staying ahead of the devil? Are you seeking revelation?

The Precipice of Time

Don't tear your clothing in your grief, but tear your hearts instead. Return to the Lord your God, for he is merciful and compassionate, slow to get angry and filled with unfailing love. He is eager to relent and not punish. Who knows? Perhaps he will give you a reprieve, sending you a blessing instead of this curse. Perhaps you will be able to offer grain and wine to the Lord your God as before (Joel 2:13-14 NLT).

TIME has many fascinating aspects; time has a beginning and it will come to an end someday. Sometimes we stand at the precipice of time. At such times, you can lean on God and make it the dawn of a new era, a time of His power and favor—or you can lean on your own understanding, which often leads to futility and failure.

It is crucial; you don't leave things to chance at such critical times! If there was ever a time to pray, then standing at the precipice of time is that time! If you discern a precipice, show unswerving commitment to God, at least by humble, prayerful submission.

This is also a time to pursue the goals and aspirations deep within your heart as inspired by the Holy Spirit. Indeed, as the Bible says, there is eternity in the hearts of every person (see Eccles. 3). What you do at these times determines your next place in God. At such a precipice, the king of Nineveh called for national repentance with fasting and prayers, saying; *"Who knows? God may yet relent and with compassion turn from his fierce anger so that we will not perish"* (Jonah 3:9 NIV). As a result God left them with a blessing instead of a curse.

Are you prepared to turn your precipice of time into a blessing instead of curse?

God's Promises Are Your Armor

He will cover you with his feathers. He will shelter you with his wings. His faithful promises are your armor and protection (Psalm 91:4 NLT).

THE promises of God have divine armor that protect, and whenever you proclaim His promises over yourself, whether the circumstance is favorable or not, you put on this wonderful armor. The word of promise from God is a protection and also has its inherent propelling power toward fulfilment.

When you dwell on His eternal Word, believe in His Word, and put on the armor of His promises, then the devil and his agents will not be able to touch you.

No matter what problems you are facing, God's protection is your saving grace. He will protect you; He will be with you; He is ever faithful.

Are you trusting Him?

The Lord has Need of It

After Jesus had said this, he went on ahead, going up to Jerusalem. As he approached Bethphage and Bethany at the hill called the Mount of Olives, he sent two of his disciples, saying to them, "Go to the village ahead of you, and as you enter it, you will find a colt tied there, which no one has ever ridden. Untie it and bring it here. If anyone asks you, 'Why are you untying it?' say, 'The Lord needs it.'" Those who were sent ahead went and found it just as he had told them. As they were untying the colt, its owners asked them, "Why are you untying the colt?" They replied, "The Lord needs it" (Luke 19:28-34).

THERE was a donkey born with a great destiny, but circumstance held her down until Jesus came its way and its story changed forever. A great destiny but it was tied!

What that donkey suffered is not an uncommon occurrence with people as well—and it often takes the presence of God for it to be realized! Jesus told His disciples to untie it because God needs it. When you decide to submit yourself and your potentials to God, no limitation can hold you down because He is obliged to untie what the enemy has done to hold you down.

When God sets you free, indeed you become free—free to accomplish your divine purpose. You will be restored to the original purpose for your life. The Lord has need of you; you were made for a divine purpose!

Are you still tied up somewhere?
What will it take for you to be loosed?

The Time of Joseph's Manifestation

There is a time for everything, and a season for every activity under the heavens (Ecclesiastes 3:1).

THERE is a time appointed for a thing to manifest. The Bible speaks of time appointed for John the Baptist to manifest, *"So the child grew and became strong in spirit, and was in the deserts till the day of his manifestation to Israel"* (Luke 1:80 NKJV).

And I introduce another time I call the time a Joseph Manifestation, *"The plan seemed good to Pharaoh and to all his officials. So Pharaoh asked them, "Can we find anyone like this man, one in whom is the spirit of God?" Then Pharaoh said to Joseph, "Since God has made all this known to you, there is no one so discerning and wise as you. You shall be in charge of my palace, and all my people are to submit to your orders. Only with respect to the throne will I be greater than you"* (Gen. 41:37-40). That was how the painful experiences of Joseph's journey were transformed to a life of power and dominance.

Many people have experienced this sudden transformation—a "Joseph Manifestation." That Joseph was gifted was never in doubt and that his father lavished love on him was equally undisputed. In his naiveté and youthful exuberance, he got on the wrong side of his brothers. He had very painful experiences, but he kept his heart of purpose and love—and one day his story changed. As for you, keep a heart of love and keep on going on, your time will surely come.

Do you believe and are you trusting that your Joseph Manifestation will come?

The Glory of His Presence

*The heavens declare the **glory of God;** the skies proclaim the work of his hands* (Psalm 19:1).

SOME of the benefits of the glory of God include: His presence, goodness, the proclamation of His name, His mercy, His compassion, and a place by Him (His secret place), the hand of God, and frequent revelation from the throne of God.

The Bible says, *"Then Moses said to him, 'If your Presence does not go with us, do not send us up from here. How will anyone know that you are pleased with me and with your people unless you go with us? What else will distinguish me and your people from all the other people on the face of the earth?' And the LORD said to Moses, 'I will do the very thing you have asked, because I am pleased with you and I know you by name.' Then Moses said, 'Now show me your glory.' And the LORD said, 'I will cause all my goodness to pass in front of you, and I will proclaim my name, the LORD, in your presence. I will have mercy on whom I will have mercy, and I will have compassion on whom I will have compassion. But,' he said, 'you cannot see my face, for no one may see me and live.' Then the LORD said, 'There is a place near me where you may stand on a rock. When my glory passes by, I will put you in a cleft in the rock and cover you with my hand until I have passed by'"* (Exodus 33:15-22). You will exhibit the glorious attributes of His presence all the days of your life.

**Have you experienced the glory
of the Lord recently? Ever?**

The Time of Transition

The effective, fervent prayer of a righteous man avails much
(James 5:16 NKJV).

THERE are places and times that memories are made of, and it is beneficial to recognize them. I believe such times and places are common, though we let many slip by. They go by without notice, and the time of prayer is one such time.

Prayer times are times of transition; meaning, prayer offers you the opportunity to connect with Heaven and transition from struggles to dominance, from lack to abundance, from mediocrity to excellence, and from sickness to health.

As a person of prayers, you will enjoy these transformations. The effective and fervent prayer of a righteous person brings about much, and surely that includes you. Indeed, as you continue a life of prayers, may your oil never stop flowing! A prayerful Christian is a powerful Christian. Prayers make the difference and connect you to the limitless power of God.

Now is the time for your transition into a place of dominance, abundance, and excellence. Yes?

The Pillar of God's Glory

When the day of Pentecost came, they were all together in one place. Suddenly a sound like the blowing of a violent wind came from heaven and filled the whole house where they were sitting (Acts 2:1-2).

THE pillar of cloud and pillar of fire that led the Israelites out of Egypt is now the fire in today's believers. This is true, and it carries no less power than the one that defeated the mighty Pharaoh of Egypt. Just imagine that a force mighty enough to defeat a world power is now within the temple of God—the body of each believer! This is how it came about. The Holy Spirit was given by God the Father to the believers on the day of the Pentecost, read Acts 2:1-4.

Exodus 40:34-38 says, *"Then the cloud covered the tent of meeting, and the glory of the LORD filled the tabernacle. Moses could not enter the tent of meeting because the cloud had settled on it, and the glory of the LORD filled the tabernacle. In all the travels of the Israelites, whenever the cloud lifted from above the tabernacle, they would set out; but if the cloud did not lift, they did not set out—until the day it lifted. **So the cloud of the LORD was over the tabernacle by day, and fire was in the cloud by night,** in the sight of all the Israelites during all their travels."*

May God's glory give you guidance and protection as you journey on this earth. Indeed, you are a walking world superpower with mighty powers in God.

In what ways do you think and act like a godly world superpower?

Reading the Bible in a Year: Genesis 31-32 & Matthew 10:24-42.

Divine Advancement and Acceleration

*For we are God's handiwork, created in Christ Jesus to do good works, which **God prepared in advance** for us to do* (Ephesians 2:10).

DIVINE advancement and acceleration are some of the ways God intervenes and brings about His purpose and an increased pace toward the fulfillment of His plans concerning you.

Pray using the following: For divine advancement, *"It was the Lord that advanced Moses and Aaron"* (1 Sam. 12:6 KJV). For divine acceleration, *"Meanwhile, the sky grew black with clouds, the wind rose, a heavy rain started falling and Ahab rode off to Jezreel. The power of the LORD came on Elijah and, tucking his cloak into his belt, he ran ahead of Ahab all the way to Jezreel"* (1 Kings 18:45-46). For a rock of escape from the enemy's trap, *"Saul and his men began the search, and when David was told about it, he went down to the rock and stayed in the Desert of Maon. When Saul heard this, he went into the Desert of Maon in pursuit of David. Saul was going along one side of the mountain, and David and his men were on the other side, hurrying to get away from Saul. As Saul and his forces were closing in on David and his men to capture them, a messenger came to Saul, saying, 'Come quickly! The Philistines are raiding the land.' Then Saul broke off his pursuit of David and went to meet the Philistines. That is why they call this place Sela Hammahlekoth"* (1 Sam. 23:25-28).

God will advance you.

In what areas of your life do you pray for advancement?

What Song Is in Your Heart?

Make a joyful shout to the LORD, all you lands! Serve the LORD with gladness; Come before His presence with singing. Know that the LORD, He is God; it is He who has made us, and not we ourselves; we are His people and the sheep of His pasture (Psalm 100:1-3 NKJV).

THIS is what the Bible says, *"For in my inner being I delight in God's law"* (Rom. 7:22). A song in your heart is the total demeanor of the state of your heart. It is the product of the experiences that you have allowed to linger on in your heart. It is the reflection of your management and perception of the events and people who came across your path in life.

A joyful song in your heart is like the sunrise of your soul, and a sad song in your heart is like the downcast of your soul. If God determines the song in your heart, then it will not depend on your circumstance. Let God dictate the song in your heart, don't leave it to anything or anybody else. No matter what song the circumstance may want to put in your heart, be steadfast in trusting God; for the joy of the Lord is your strength.

May you wake up morning by morning with a joyful song in your heart. May such songs as "To God be the glory for great things He has done. Praise the Lord, praise the Lord, let the people rejoice, let the earth praise His name" linger in your heart. No matter what evil the day may hold, may these songs testify in your life and everywhere you go.

What song is in your heart?

Reading the Bible in a Year: Genesis 36-37 & Matthew 12:1-21.

Someone Is Praying for You

I have not stopped giving thanks for you, remembering you in my prayers (Ephesians 1:16).

SOMETIMES we experience an unexpected turn of good fortune; like being rescued from a situation that others did not make it through. One of the reasons this often happens is because someone is praying for us. Sometimes, the only way we got to our present position in life was because someone somewhere was committed to praying for us.

The prophet Samuel said, *"For the sake of his great name the LORD will not reject his people, because the LORD was pleased to make you his own. As for me, **far be it from me that I should sin against the LORD by failing to pray for you.** And I will teach you the way that is good and right"* (1 Sam. 12:22-23). Paul said; *"For this reason when I could stand it no longer, I sent to find out about your faith. I was afraid that in some way the tempter might have tempted you and our labors might have been in vain!"* (1 Thess. 3:5). Here Paul expresses the fear and desire of any true shepherd or parent.

You need a good prayer life as well as the prayer of the saints to stay above all the wiles of the devil! Let me be that someone to pray for you today; I pray that the grace of God in your life will not be in vain. May God establish the work of your hands. May the Lord bless your work produced by faith, your labor prompted by love, and your tirelessness inspired by hope in our Lord Jesus. May your heart be strengthened by grace through Jesus Christ and may the God of peace equip you with everything good for doing His will. This is my prayer for you today.

What is your prayer today?

Egyptians Today— Gone Tomorrow

*Moses answered the people, "**Do not be afraid**. Stand firm and you will see the deliverance the LORD will bring you today. The Egyptians you see today you will never see again. **The LORD will fight for you**; you need only to be still"*
(Exodus 14:13-14).

THIS was a metaphoric illustration by Moses. The Egyptians were problems to the Israelites at the time, so Moses symbolically says that the problems will never be seen by them again. All the Israelites needed to do was hold their peace.

Often the most difficult time to be still is when we are under diverse trials and facing hard problems. Yet, this is when we need to put aside agitation, anxiety, and worries! In quietness and rest is our strength. Stillness does not mean lack of activities, it means calmness on the inside despite the challenges on the outside.

Yes, often we need to be reminded to be still and know that He is God. May the essence of this resonate in your spirit and may you wake up in the morning with this stillness in your heart. The Bible says; *"Be still and know that I am God, I will be exalted among the nations; I will be exalted in the earth. The Lord Almighty is with us; the God of Jacob is our fortress!"* (Ps. 46:10-11).

How easy is it for you to be still?

That the Lord May Exalt You

Like your name, O God, your praise reaches to the ends of the earth; your right hand is filled with righteousness. For this God is our God forever and ever; He will be our guide even to the end (Psalm 48:10,14).

WHATEVER you do today remember this, humble yourself in the hands of Almighty God and He will surely exalt you! Show someone some goodness and love. Then show someone else too. As for goodness, it overcomes evil; and for love, it never fails. Arm yourself with these weapons and failure will be far from you today and every day!

Love is patient, love is kind. It does not envy, it does not boast, it is not proud. It does not dishonor others, it is not self-seeking, it is not easily angered, it keeps no record of wrongs. Love does not delight in evil but rejoices with the truth. It always protects, always trusts, always hopes, always perseveres. Love never fails... (1 Corinthians 13:4-8).

Is this definition of love close to yours?

The Peace of God

*And **the peace of God, which transcends all understanding, will guard your hearts and your minds** in Christ Jesus. Finally, brothers and sisters, whatever is true, whatever is noble, whatever is right, whatever is pure, whatever is lovely, whatever is admirable—if anything is excellent or praiseworthy—think about such things. Whatever you have learned or received or heard from me, or seen in me—put it into practice. And **the God of peace will be with you*** (Philippians 4:7-9).

GOD is the Father of glory and He imparts His glory to our spirits with great peace. Peace is our silent weapon, and the glory of God in our lives is the nature of God manifested through us. Peace as one of the aspects of the glory of God is exhibited when we enjoy the peace of God that surpasses all understanding. The glory of God and peace of God are therefore interwoven and as such we enjoy dual benefits when we tap into the peace of God.

The peace of God that passes understanding will from this day be imputed to you; as the Bible says, *"The kingdom of God is not a matter of eating and drinking but of righteousness, **peace** and joy in the Holy Spirit"* (Rom. 14:17). The art of maintaining godly peace is a deliberate and a conscientious effort that everyone has to make. Indeed, God keeps in perfect peace those whose hearts are focused on Him.

By the grace of God that perfect peace comes; our responsibility is to ensure our heart stays on Him. Colossians 3:15 says, *"Let the peace of Christ rule in your hearts, since as members of one body you were called to peace. And be thankful."* May you experience the great peace of God, and may you feel the manifest presence of the God of peace living within you from today and forever!

Can you describe the peace that passes all understanding?

Reading the Bible in a Year: Genesis 44-45 & Matthew 14:1-21.

Granted! Victory over Every Lie!

If any nation [thing] *comes to fight [trouble, harass intimidate] you, it is not because I sent them. Therefore it will be routed, for I am on your side...no weapon turned against you shall succeed and you will have justice against every courtroom lie* (Isaiah 54:15-17 Living Bible).

G OD is the Revealer of secrets; and when His light comes, any darkness in whatever form dissipates. This includes any lie in whatever level of court or gossip circle it exists. It will be exposed by God to whom nothing is hidden.

The Bible verse from Isaiah is to bless and remind you of the goodness of your God. God will lead you to the rock that is higher than you are! Our times are in God's hands, He will help us at the break of this and every day! Every lie will be exposed and defeated.

**Have you been a victim of a vicious lie?
Believe that God will expose it.**

The God of Jacob Is Our Fortress

*...I will be exalted among the nations; I will be exalted in the earth. The Lord Almighty is with us; the God of Jacob is our **fortress!** (Psalm 46:10-11)*

THE Bible is clear that God is to be our fortress. We are protected from harm when we use Him as our fort—our stronghold.

*He said: "The LORD is my rock, my **fortress** and my deliverer* (2 Samuel 22:2). May the truth in this verse play out in your life this day!

*The LORD is my rock, my **fortress** and my deliverer; my God is my rock, in whom I take refuge, my shield and the horn of my salvation, my stronghold* (Psalm 18:2).

*Turn your ear to me, come quickly to my rescue; be my rock of refuge, a strong **fortress** to save me* (Psalm 31:2).

*Whoever fears the LORD has a secure **fortress**, and for their children it will be a refuge* (Proverbs 14:26).

What do you think of when you hear or see the word fortress? Is God your Fortress?

Special Skills to Accomplish His Plans

Also I have given ability to all the skilled workers to make everything I have commanded you (Exodus 31:6).

Bless all his skills, LORD, *and be pleased with the work of his hands. Strike down those who rise against him, his foes till they rise no more* (Deuteronomy 33:11).

S KILL means the ability to successfully accomplish something that requires special knowledge or a certain level of proficiency. Skills are built from the potentials given by God and require humankind cooperating with God to bring this to practical realities.

May God grant you special grace and skills as He granted Bezalel and Oholiab; they were filled with great wisdom, intelligence, and skills for their time and season!

Then the LORD said to Moses, "See, I have chosen Bezalel son of Uri, the son of Hur, of the tribe of Judah, and I have filled him with the Spirit of God, with wisdom, with understanding, with knowledge and with all kinds of skills—to make artistic designs for work in gold, silver and bronze, to cut and set stones, to work in wood, and to engage in all kinds of crafts. Moreover, I have appointed Oholiab son of Ahisamak, of the tribe of Dan, to help him (Exodus 31:1-5).

What special skills did the Lord give you?

The Lord God of the Hebrews

The elders of Israel will listen to you. Then you and the
elders are to go to the king of Egypt and say to him, 'The
***LORD, the God of the Hebrews**, has met with us. Let us*
take a three-day journey into the wilderness to offer
sacrifices to the LORD our God (Exodus 3:18).

GOD told Moses to say to Pharaoh that the Lord God of the
Hebrews sent him (see verse above). This is the special attribute of God's sovereignty in action; that He has a chosen people, a
peculiar people, and has translated them into a special position that
marks them out from other people.

The Psalmist says, *"Know that the Lord is God. It is He who made*
us and we are his people, the sheep of his pasture" (Ps. 100:3)—the
apple of His eyes.

Let us have faith and be prepared to witness the full dynamics
of the power of the Lord God of the Hebrews fighting for you! I pray
that God would rend the heavens and come down and do awesome
miracles in your midst!

Come Lord, Your children are waiting!

Is the Lord God of the Hebrews your God as well?

Prayers for the Season's Blessings

*Moses replied, "When I have gone out of the city, **I will spread out my hands in prayer to the LORD.** The thunder will stop and there will be no more hail, so you may know that the earth is the LORD's* (Exodus 9:29).

Today and tomorrow, I offer the following Scriptures and proclamations to shower you with His faithfulness. Take them to heart and think about them seriously.

1. You shall possess your possession, even as the sons of Jacob possessed their possessions!

God will arise and let His enemies will be scattered! *"May God arise, may his enemies be scattered; may his foes flee before him"* (Ps. 68.1).

2. You shall overcome by the blood of the Lamb and the word of your testimony! *"Then war broke out in heaven. ...The great dragon was hurled down—that ancient serpent called the devil, or Satan, who leads the whole world astray. He was hurled to the earth, and his angels with him. Then I heard a loud voice in heaven say: 'Now have come the salvation and the power and the kingdom of our God, and the authority of his Messiah. For the accuser of our brothers and sisters, who accuses them before our God day and night, has been hurled down. They triumphed over him by the blood of the Lamb and by the word of their testimony; they did not love their lives so much as to shrink from death'"* (Rev. 12:7-11).

Your enemies will be scattered and you will overcome. Do you believe this?

Prayers for the Season's Blessings, continued

*"It is written," he said to them, '**My house will be a house of prayer**'"* (Luke 19:46).

Prayers are the means to tap into the blessings of God, the essential ingredients of the fulfilment of blessings.

I stand on the Word of God that His promises will be manifested in your life.

3. God will grant you rest on all sides! *"So the LORD gave Israel all the land he had sworn to give their ancestors, and they took possession of it and settled there. The LORD gave them rest on every side, just as he had sworn to their ancestors. Not one of their enemies withstood them; the LORD gave all their enemies into their hands"* (Josh. 21:43-44).

4. None of God's good promises concerning you shall fail! *"Not one of all the LORD's good promises to Israel failed; every one was fulfilled"* (Josh. 21:45).

God will grant you rest, and His promises never fail.
Do you believe this?

Feasting in the Presence of Enemies

*You prepare a table before me in the presence of my enemies.
You anoint my head with oil; my cup overflows. Surely your
goodness and love will follow me all the days of my life, and
I will dwell in the house of the LORD forever* (Psalm 23:5-6).

HAVE you ever wondered why God would not first get rid of the
enemies before preparing a table for you? The answer is that He
delights in showing Himself strong in the full view of the enemies so
that the glory will come to Him and Him alone.

So the presence of a very strong enemy is not always bad news,
it could be an occasion for God to display His power in your life. It
may be the sign that you have entered the beginning of the reign of
His power in you against all who have stood against you in the past.
In fact, it could be the beginning of the demonstration of His glory in
your life in a new and fresh way!

Be ready to feed at His banquet in full view of your enemies. For
this God is our God, He will forever remain your Shepherd; and from
now on, no good thing will be withheld from you!

**How hard is it for you to believe that the presence of
a very strong enemy is not always bad news?**

The Glory and the Lifter of Your Head

Many are saying of me, "God will not deliver him." But you, LORD, are a shield around me, my glory, the One who lifts my head high (Psalm 3:2-3).

THE Bible says the crippled man at the beautiful gate jumped up with a leap and started walking, leaping, and praising God (see Acts 3:1-10). May your story also change for the good—that you will bounce out of your limitation and be restored to His glorious and victorious life!

May you always have an awesome time in the presence of the Lord! He is your glory and the lifter up of your head. Be expecting eternal weight of glory to be released upon you and surely the King of glory will Himself tabernacle with you!

Are you ready for some leaping and praising God?

Reading the Bible in a Year: Exodus 13-15 & Matthew 19:1-15.

The Name above All Others

God exalted Him to the highest place and gave Him the name is above every name, that at the name of Jesus every knee should bow, in heaven and on earth and under the earth (Philippians 2:9-10).

M AY this truth be realized in your life today and for evermore!

Before attaining the name above all other names, Jesus humbled Himself, endured ridicule and suffering! Often the way to stand above all others is first of all the way of humility.

For to us a child is born, to us a son is given, and the government will be on his shoulders. And he will be called Wonderful Counselor, Mighty God, Everlasting Father, Prince of Peace. Of the greatness of his government and peace there will be no end (Isaiah 9:6-7).

May this passage be realized in your life today and for evermore!

What is your favorite other name for Jesus?

Rejoice Always in the Lord

Rejoice in the Lord always. I will say it again: Rejoice!
(Philippians 4:4)

THIS admonition from Apostle Paul asks us to deliberately make efforts to be joyful and maintain the peace of God in the inside, because therein lies our strength.

Let the peace of God rule your heart and mind! This is the key to living a life without fear.

Speaking to one another with psalms, hymns and songs from the Spirit. Sing and make music from your heart to the Lord, always giving thanks to God the Father for everything, in the name of our Lord Jesus Christ (Ephesians 5:19- 20).

Remember it is with joy that you can draw water from the well of salvation, *"With joy you will draw water from the wells of salvation"* (Isa. 12:3). Your miracle is nearer than you think! The prophet Isaiah declares, *"Tell the righteous it will be well with them, for they will enjoy the fruit of their deeds"* (Isa. 3:10).

How rejoiceful are you?

The Midnight Hour

At midnight I rise to give you thanks for your righteous laws
(Psalm 119:62).

E VERY midnight hour is a time and chance to enter a new and bet-ter day—perhaps the dawn of a brighter future! You shall enter a new day, *"with singing; everlasting joy will crown your heads; gladness and joy will overtake you and sorrow and sighing will flee away"* (Isa. 35:10), from now and forever!

There is nothing to fear at the midnight hour, this is time when other gods are sleeping; but our God is always awake, He never sleeps. It was at the midnight hour He delivered Paul and Silas; and was at the midnight hour His agent of death passed over the Israelites but brought death to the Egyptians.

As you cross over your next midnight hour, may the Lord arise on your behalf *"as He did at Mount Perazim, He will rouse Himself as in the Valley of Gibeon to do His work"* (Isa. 28:21), and fight your battles! May you plunder the Egyptians—your problems—and move into your overflow anointing loaded with abundance and divine sub-stance! May today and your tomorrows be bright.

How fearful are you of night time?
Are you prepared to welcome Him then?

There is Nothing to Fear

*The Spirit you received does not make you slaves, so that
you live in fear again; rather, the Spirit you received brought
about your adoption to sonship. And by him we cry,
"Abba, Father"* (Romans 8:15).

FAITH is the opposite of fear. Prayers and the word of God drive out fear by increasing faith. Let the following verses build up your faith. In Second Timothy 1:7, *"For God has not given us the spirit of fear, but of power, and of love and of a sound mind"* and Acts 4:24, *"they raised their voices together in prayer to God,"* and God answered with miraculous signs and wonders!

The prophet Isaiah said, *"In righteousness you will be established: tyranny will be far from you; you will have nothing to fear. ...whoever attacks you, will surrender to you"* (Isa. 54:14-15).

The Bible also says faith comes by hearing the word of God, so build up yourself by not forsaking the assembly of the saints. As faith builds up, it calls forth things! Let faith arise; *"what is seen was not made out of what was visible"* (Heb. 11:3).

Do you have anything that needs to be called forth?

Preparing a Feast of Rich Food

On this mountain the Lord Almighty will prepare a feast of rich food for all peoples, a banquet of aged wines—the best of meats and the finest of wines (Isaiah 25:6).

GOD is always eager to bless and bless abundantly. And it is true that a sumptuous feast such as described above is the desire of God for you; but to participate in this feast, we need humility and repentance! So prepare yourself with prayer and cry out to the Lord with this: *"wash away all my iniquity and cleanse me from my sin"* (Ps. 51:2).

That is why the bible says, *"in repentance and rest is your salvation, in quietness and trust is your strength"* (Isa. 30:15).

As you do this, *"May the LORD, the God of your ancestors, increase you a thousand times and bless you as He has promised!"* (Deut. 1:11). That was the prayer of Moses over the Jews as they were poised to enter the Promised Land—and this is my prayer for you today.

Are you sitting at His table in humility and repentance?

An Everlasting Covenant

I have set my rainbow in the clouds, and it will be the sign of the covenant between me and the earth (Genesis 9:13).

THE rainbow is a sign of covenant and it was the seal of Noahic covenant; the covenant of second chance! Covenants are important and God is a covenant keeping God.

This was King David's declaration about his family: *"And it is my family He has chosen! Yes, God has made an everlasting covenant with me; His agreement is eternal, final, sealed. He will constantly look after my safety and success!"* (2 Samuel 23:5 Living Bible).

The same shall apply to you and your family!

It is God who arms me with strength and keeps my way secure. He makes my feet like the feet of a deer; he causes me to stand on the heights. He trains my hands for battle; my arms can bend a bow of bronze. You make your saving help my shield; your help has made me great (2 Samuel 22:33-36).

This is a season for equipping for everyone and every church worker. "Church workers" means those who work for the Body of Christ, and that includes you. This is your portion as you wake up to the dawn of a new day!

**Have you accepted with gratefulness
God's eternal covenant?**

The Vision Is for an Appointed Time

From one man he made all the nations, that they should inhabit the whole earth; and he marked out their appointed times in history and the boundaries of their lands
(Acts 17:26).

THIS is reassuring! Then it means that the geography of our place of birth and even the eventual place of our abode have not come about by chance. I want you to know for sure that the vision concerning you is for an appointed time!

> *"Slowly, steadily, surely, the time approaches when the vision will be fulfilled. If it seems slow, do not despair, for these things will surely come to pass. Just be patient! They will not be overdue a single day!"* (Habakkuk 2:3b Living Bible).

God makes everything beautiful in its time. This also should be your daily reminder! He that promised is faithful and well able to perform it.

Are you expecting your appointed time to arrive right on time?

There Is a Way Out

No temptation has overtaken you except what is common to mankind. And God is faithful; he will not let you be tempted beyond what you can bear. But when you are tempted, ***he will also provide a way out*** *so that you can endure it* (1 Corinthians 10:13).

THERE is a way out of any situation for those who put their trust in Him!

Be encouraged by this story: four lepers were once surrounded by death on every conceivable side, but God quickened them to the path of life in the midst of their crippling possibilities. They said, *"Why stay here until we die?"* (2 Kings 7:3b).

This is my decree for you; you will not die but live. Instead of death, the lepers entered into their deliverance, prosperity, abundance, and they even brought victory to their nation!

Your next step of faith will lead to a resounding victory.

When looking for a way out, are you looking for God?

Destroy Complacency and Advance

For even when we were with you, we gave you this rule: "The one who is unwilling to work shall not eat." We hear that some among you are idle and disruptive. They are not busy; they are busybodies (2 Thessalonians 3:10-11).

THE spirit of complacency is a hindrance to the ability to break from the unwanted monotony of repeated routines. By prayers the evil of complacency can be broken. As the Bible says. *"Men ought always to pray and not cease"*! And also that, *"The fervent and effective prayers of the righteous man avail much."*

By prayers and submission to God you will prompted to break the spirit of complacency. In His presence and under His guidance, God said to Israelites, *"You have stayed long enough at this mountain. Break camp and advance"* (Deut. 1:6). You, too, will break out of your routine and move into the miraculous!

Later God also said to them, *"See, I have given you this land. Go in and take possession of the land"* (Deut. 1:8). The same thing I believe God is saying to you today. Never give up, Your victory is assured! This is your time and your season to take what belongs to you! Break up your fallow ground and break up your complacency.

What steps can you take right now to break up your complacency?

The Lord Is Your Shepherd

The Lord is my shepherd. I lack nothing. He makes me lie down in green pastures, He leads me beside quiet waters [the waters of life], He refreshes my soul (Psalm 23:1-3a).

SOMETIMES, the words of a very familiar Bible passage lift up off the page of the Bible and ignite something inside. This is part of the phenomena called *rhema,* a birthing in the spirit or a quickening in the inner being. This is why the Bible is referred to as the living Word of God!

I have had the very familiar passage Psalm 23 ignite something in my inner being, and I have been so greatly impacted. Then I wondered, *How can something so familiar be so profoundly uplifting?*

I pray you that this will happen each time you read the Bible. Out of the routines can come something great! May He awaken your ears to His *now* word morning by morning.

How can something so familiar ignite your inner self as if reading for the first time?

God's Flames of Fire

Therefore, since we are receiving a kingdom that cannot be shaken, let us be thankful, and so worship God acceptably with reverence and awe, for **our "God is a consuming fire"**
(Hebrews 12:28-29).

WHAT a privilege we have to be counted usable by God! The Book of Acts says: *"there appeared unto them cloven tongues* [separated tongues or more than one but joined] *like as of fire and it sat upon each of them"* (Acts 2:3 KJV). This is the fire in each believer; each has become God's flame of fire.

Speaking about the fire inherent in the word of God, the prophet Jeremiah said, *"his word is in my heart like a **fire**, a **fire** shut up in my **bones"** (Jer. 20:9). My prayer for you as a child and minister of God is for you to become a flame of fire, spreading His Word near and far.

Are you on fire for God?

New Every Morning

*Because of the LORD's great love we are not consumed, for his
compassions never fail. They are new every morning; great is
your faithfulness* (Lamentations 3:22-23).

Mᴀʏ the Lord always drop something refreshing in your spirit every morning. He awakens my ears to His word every morning.

Sometime ago, early in the morning, God dropped this in my spirit: prepare for the manifestation of Joseph and Daniel's blessings! What are the key features of these blessings? They include uncommon wisdom, excellence in the land of your sojourn, favor with strangers, promotion from earthly authorities, and economic and spiritual dominion.

**Does God's love and compassions
greet you every morning?**

Breaking the Curse of a Barren Land

The seed will grow well, the vine will yield its fruit, the ground will produce its crops and the heavens will drops their dews (Zechariah 8:12).

THE above was the result of the breaking of the curse of the land incurred in the Book of Haggai; *"Therefore because of you, the heavens have withheld their dew and the earth its crops"* (Haggai 1:10).

As you pray today, pray for every situation around you, your family, and your land—that they will bring forth increase and to break the curse of bareness from its root source.

This is the story of how Elisha broke the curse of barrenness that was upon Jericho, *"Then he went out to the **source of the water,** and cast in the salt there, and said, 'Thus says the Lord: I have healed this water; from it there shall be no more death or bareness'"* (2 Kings 2:21 NKJV).

God will address the source of your water to make it wholesome forever! May your land never be unproductive again.

Are you ready for your land, family, and every situation to be productive and fruitful?

Season of the Miraculous

There is a time for everything, and a season for every activity under the heavens (Ecclesiastes 3:1).

A season is any period of time suitable or convenient or favorable for something. Season therefore implies opportunity is available.

May you move into the season of the miraculous, destiny, and advancement. It shall be according to the original blueprint of God for your life: nothing missing, nothing broken!

There is also a season of prophetic declaration into your life: *"By a prophet the LORD brought Israel out of Egypt, and by a prophet was he* [Israel] *preserved"* (Hos. 12:13 KJV). *"The elders of the Jews continued to build and prosper under the preaching* [prophesying] *of Haggai"* (Ezra 6:14a). Have you sought it out?

So it shall be for you. May all these blessings characterize this season in your life.

Are you expecting the unexpected?

Sacrifice of Thanksgiving

"I have no need of a bull from your stall or of goats from your pens, for every animal of the forest is mine, and the cattle on a thousand hills. I know every bird in the mountains.... If I were hungry, I would not tell you, for the world is mine, and all that is in it. Sacrifice thank offerings to God, fulfill your vows to the Most High" (Psalm 50:9-14).

I believe God was saying, "What I want from you is your true thanks." Sacrifice is giving up something for something considered to be more valuable.

Today, offer to the Lord the sacrifice of thanksgiving, no matter the circumstance you may find yourself.

Come to the Lord today with a thankful heart! If He has not been on your side, the enemy would have swallowed you!

Thanks be to God!

Have you made any significant sacrifices for God lately?

The Feast of Esther

For if you [Esther] *remain silent at this time, relief and deliverance for the Jews will arise from another place, but you and your father's family will perish. And who knows but that you have come to your royal position for such a time as this?"*
(Esther 4:14)

ESTHER had a national celebration named after her—The Feast of Esther! That is how blessed she was. So blessed that she was a blessing to many other people, even the entire nation! *"She* [Esther] *obtained grace and favor in his* [the king's] *sight...so he set the royal crown upon her head and made her queen instead of Vashti. Then the king made a great feast, the Feast of Esther...and he proclaimed a holiday...and gave gifts according to the generosity of a king"* (Esther 2:17-18).

Esther was remarkable! She was extremely beautiful, but kept her obedience to Mordecai. She was promoted to the palace, but did not forget her humble roots! Esther prevailed against the evil plans of Haman and power changed hands from Haman to Mordecai and the Jews.

This is your portion! I pray that great grace will be available for you to do His purpose.

Remembering Esther's courage to stand before the king, are you willing to stand before others and speak the name of Christ?

Reading the Bible in a Year: Leviticus 14 & Matthew 26:55-75.

Deliverance Comes from the Lord

Then Esther sent this reply to Mordecai: "Go, gather together all the Jews who are in Susa, and fast for me. Do not eat or drink for three days, night or day. I and my attendants will fast as you do. When this is done, I will go to the king, even though it is against the law. And if I perish, I perish" (Esther 4:15-16).

THERE is always the chance of a divine breakthrough—no matter what!

Once there was an evil order to destroy, kill, and annihilate all the Jews. But Mordecai tore his clothes and put on sackcloth and ashes when he heard of it. Then he said to Esther, *"if you remain silent at this time, relief and deliverance for the Jews will arise from another place"* (Esther 4:14).

Mordecai refused to give up! And God turned the table against their enemies (see Esther 9:1). Truly, it is not over until it is over! Never give up on your dreams; help can come from "another place." Be encouraged today; God is standing with you! You will not fail. The Bible says, "You are blessed and highly favored!" (Luke 1:28).

Do you keep your God-options open, ready to accept His help?

Emmanuel—The Lord Is with You

Peace I [Jesus] leave with you; my peace I give you. I do not give to you as the world gives. Do not let your hearts be troubled and do not be afraid (John 14:27).

THEN I am reminded of Emmanuel in the Book of Genesis, *"I am with you and will watch over you wherever you go, and I will bring you back to this land. I will not leave you until I have done what I have promised you"* (Gen. 28:15). As He promised Jacob then, He is promising you today.

Again there is Emmanuel in the Book of Exodus; *"If Your Presence does not go with us, do not bring us up from here"* (Exod. 33:15). Moses knew then as we know now, His presence is all that matters.

Be assured today that no matter where you are, He is all about you, you are very special, He covers you with His shadow, you dwell in the secret place of the Most High, never forget that.

Do you believe in your heart, mind, and spirit that
God is with you always?

The Prophetic Promise

We also have the prophetic message as something completely reliable, and you will do well to pay attention to it, as to a light shining in a dark place, until the day dawns and the morning star rises in your hearts (2 Peter 1:19).

THIS is what apostle Peter said regarding the prophetic word you have received. The Living Bible puts it this way, *"But when you consider the wonderful truth of the prophet's words, then the light will dawn in your soul and Christ the Morning Star will shine in your hearts"* (2 Peter 1:19b). The prophetic promise can be your source of peace in times of trouble!

Surely the Word of God will do you good! This is the wisdom of the moment: *"as far as it depends on you, live at peace with everyone"* (Rom. 12:18). Please bear this in mind so you don't react violently to situations, no matter the provocation, but respond from your place in God. In this way, you will not miss your blessing! Amen.

How easy is it for you to be at peace with all people?

"That Day"

> On **that day** the LORD will shield those who live in Jeru-
> salem, so that the feeblest among them will be like David,
> and the house of David will be like God, like the angel of the
> LORD going before them. On **that day** I will set out to destroy
> all the nations that attack Jerusalem (Zechariah 12:8-9).

THE Bible speaks of "that day," and we ought to grasp its importance so we appropriate all that it encompasses. Jerusalem is
your portion in the name of Jesus, my dear friend! I call you friend
because you are my friend and my prayer partner! I want you to know
that everything built on God will stand the test of time.

Be encouraged today, for *"Dear friend, I pray that you may enjoy
good health and that all may go well with you, even as your soul is getting along well"* (3 John 2). He who promised is faithful and able to do
all that concerns you. Live by the standards of the gospel and always
work for the common good of all.

Your expectations will not be cut short!

Is *that day* today in your spirit?

All of Life Is Spiritual

The Spirit of God has made me; the breath of the Almighty gives me life (Job 33:4).

PAUL admonished the Galatians and asked a crucial question, *"After beginning with the Spirit, are you now trying to attain your goal by human effort?"* (Gal. 3:3b NIV 1984).

Apostle John said, *"On the Lord's Day I was in the Spirit"* (Rev. 1:10a); then and then only was he able to receive the great message of the Book of Revelation.

As the Bible says, *if you walk by the spirit you will not gratify the desires of the flesh* (see Gal. 5:16). My prayer for you today is that your words and actions will be born of the Spirit no matter what, and that you yield a bountiful harvest!

Remember this always: His grace has brought you this far, and grace will see you through. Amen.

Are you walking in the spirit?

Mother's Day

Children, obey your parents in the Lord, for this is right.
"Honor your father and mother"—which is the first com-
mandment with a promise—"so that it may go well with
you and that you may enjoy long life on the earth"
(Ephesians 6:1-3).

THIS is a timeless truth: "the hands that rock the cradle rules the world." The expression of inherited potential is often conditioned by the circumstances in which the child grows up. This is why Paul wrote, "I am reminded of your sincere faith, which first lived in your grandmother Lois and in your mother Eunice and, I am persuaded, now lives in you also" (2 Tim. 1:5).

No doubt fathers are important, but equal importance cannot be taken from mothers. Mothers shape the world of today and tomorrow! I salute mothers this day and every day of the Lord.

Do you honor your mother? If a mother, are you honored and treated with respect?

The Key of David

...These are the words of Him who is holy and true, who holds the key of David. What He opens no one can shut, and what He shuts no one can open. I know your deeds. See, I have placed before you an open door that no one can shut. ...I will make those who are of the synagogue of Satan...come and fall down at your feet and acknowledge that I have loved you"
(Revelation 3:7-9).

THIS is a great key in our walk on earth. We need know by the might of God walking in our lives that any door that He opens no person can shut.

Jesus Christ, who is of the lineage of David, has given us the key of David. There is another feature of this key; it is a "master key." Before the advent of 'key card entry system', every large building had a key that opened every door—a master key. This key of David's functions like that. It will open any door that has been shut against you. If you can believe this, it will happen for you. Amen!

How tightly are you holding on to this key?

Omens of the Boasters will Fail

"causing the omens of the boasters to fail, making fools out of diviners" (Isaiah 44:25a NASB).

BOASTERS are people or circumstances that speaks failure to you to intimidate and take away your hope for the future and breaks your trust in God. Boasters don't know God or what God can do!

God will frustrate the plans of the enemy. The same God says that you will not lack because He is your Shepherd. To cap these blessings, He has released mighty forces on your behalf, *"These are the horns that scattered Judah, so that no one could raise their head, but the craftsmen* [divine] *have come to terrify them..."* (Zech. 1:21b).

Whatever evil that might have stopped others before you, shall not succeed against you!

Are you confident that God will frustrate your enemies?

Move Forward!

The Lord our God spoke to us in Horeb, saying 'You have dwelt long enough at this mountain" (Deuteronomy 1:6).

Therefore repent and return, so that your sins may be wiped away, in order that times of refreshing may come from the presence of the Lord (Acts 3:19).

IN some countries, the clock is adjusted twice annually. When it springs forward, everyone makes an effort to align with the time advance. At such times, they understand the times and seasons and so gain the command of their circumstances to align with the generally acknowledged chromos time.

People at this time are like *"the children of Issaachar, which were men* [and women] *that had **understanding of the times,** to know what Israel ought to do; the heads of them were two hundred; and all their brethren were at their commandment"* (1 Chron. 12:32 KJV).

Most forward movements are progressive steps. Not moving forward in itself is not a bad thing, but it must be coupled with godliness so that you know when to move forward. This is the advantage that the sons of Issaachar had over the people.

May you understand your timing and so gain forward movement

Are you keeping track of the times?

Christ, Your Passover Lamb

For Christ, our Passover lamb, has been sacrificed. Therefore let us keep the Festival, not with the old bread leavened with malice and wickedness, but with the unleavened bread of sincerity and truth (1 Corinthians 5:7-8).

P ASSOVER is a special season—the season when everything negative, ungodly, and harmful will pass over you and your household!

Passover is a season of passing over from the restrictions of human reality into the singleness of Christo-centered simplicity of life in Christ with its abundant grace and unlimited resources. As we apply the blood of the Passover Lamb we also gain exception from any plague, no matter the cause:

Now the blood shall be a sign for you on the houses where you are. And when I see the blood, I will pass over you; and the plague shall not be on you to destroy you when I strike the land of Egypt. So this day shall be to you a memorial; and you shall keep it as a feast to the LORD throughout your generations. You shall keep it as a feast by an everlasting ordinance (Exodus 12:13-14 NKJV).

**What does Jesus as the Passover Lamb
mean to you?**

The Day of Power

*Your right hand, O LORD, is majestic in **power**, Your right hand, O LORD, shatters the enemy* (Exodus 15:6 NASB).

T HERE is a day described in the Bible as the day of power (Ps. 110:3). It is a day that everything and person will agree with your godly intention and is the day everything will fall into place. All resistance will melt away!

Meditate on this day of power as you prepare for the next move of God in your life. *"Thy people shall be willing"* (Ps. 110:3 KJV) is my stand; all those connected with your case shall be willing to favor you from this day! Kings shall compete to favor you and people and kings shall be drawn to your uprising (see Isa. 60:1-3).

Therefore, arise and shine—for His glory has covered your nakedness.

What more can you do if you know God provides the power?

With God, Nothing Is Impossible

*Then the disciples came to Jesus in private and asked, "Why couldn't we drive it out?" He replied, "Because you have so little faith. Truly I tell you, **if you have faith** as small as a mustard seed, you can say to this mountain, 'Move from here to there,' and it will move. **Nothing will be impossible for you***" (Matthew 17:19-21).

THE angel told Mary, *"Elizabeth your relative has also conceived a son in her old age; and this is now the sixth month for her who was called barren. For **with God nothing will be impossible**"* (Luke 1:36-37 NKJV).

No matter the circumstances confronting you, God says He will break any area of barrenness in your life and give you a new name, the original and real name—blessed!

Everyone gave up on Elizabeth ever having a child, but God did not; His plan never fails. You will not fail; you will fulfill your purpose in life any how, any way He sees your willingness.

Are you expecting the impossible?

Quench the Evil, Fiery Darts

Above all, taking the shield of faith with which you will be able to quench all the fiery darts of the wicked one
(Ephesians 6:16).

THIS is for you today: God says, "Quench the evil, fiery darts."

The shield of faith relies on the Lord who delivered or helped you in the past to do it again!

Stand firm always! You are the one to put off the fiery challenges of the enemy and God Almighty will back you up.

I stand with you, and the Lord will help you again.

How can you quench the fiery darts?

Pray for Wisdom, Acceptance, and Protection

Wisdom's instruction is to fear the LORD, and humility comes before honor (Proverbs 15:33).

WISDOM is being able to apply the Word of God in your life. Spiritual *acceptance* is putting on the fragrance of Christ accompanied by the favor and mercy of God. *Protection* is abiding in the shadow of Almighty God, dwelling in His secret place. Pray for wisdom, acceptance, and protection for servants of God as they travel around the world to progress the Kingdom of God.

As you pray for these things, God will give double honor for all your trouble as it says in the Book of Isaiah 61:7, *"Instead of your shame you will receive a double portion honor, and instead of disgrace you will rejoice in your inheritance. And so you will inherit a double portion in your land, and everlasting joy will be yours."*

Pray for acceptance of your ministry, too (see 1 Sam. 3:19-20); that the Lord will continue to be with you; none of your words will fall to the ground, and that all the people will attest that you are sent by God.

How do you gain wisdom by the Word of God?

Redemption Completed

Later, knowing that everything had now been finished, and so that Scripture would be fulfilled, Jesus said, "I am thirsty." A jar of wine vinegar was there, so they soaked a sponge in it, put the sponge on a stalk of the hyssop plant, and lifted it to Jesus' lips. When he had received the drink, Jesus said, "It is finished." With that, he bowed his head and gave up his spirit (John 19:28-30).

JESUS said, *"It is finished."* This is the day He completely paid off all your debts, including eternal death, the punishment of fallen humankind. This is divine exchange working on your behalf. You are free from everything that hinders you from being who God intended.

Indeed, *"having wiped out the handwriting of the requirements that was against us, which was contrary to us. And He has taken it out of the way, having nailed it to the cross. Having disarmed principalities and powers He made public spectacle of them triumphing over them in it"* (Col. 2:14-15 NKJV).

Together let us proclaim indeed, "It is finished!"

Have you recently thanked God the Father and God the Son for your redemption through the cross?

God's Word—
A Hammer that Breaks Rocks

"Is not my word like fire," declares the LORD, "and like a hammer that breaks a rock in pieces?" (Jeremiah 23:29)

THE Bible says the Word of God is like a hammer that breaks a rock to pieces!

Today, if there is any rock of resistance in your way, speak the Word of God, and it will accomplish what you say. The prophet Hosea says, *"Take words with you and return to the Lord"* (Hosea 14:2). They who know their God shall be made strong to do exploits. This is your portion in Jesus' name!

Greater is He who is in you than he that is in the world! As you proclaim the Word of God in the routines of your life, the days of heaven on earth will come upon you. Today is the day Jesus taught His disciples to pray for.

**Are you using God's Word to crush
the rocks making you stumble?**

Happy New Beginning

...Rule over the fish in the sea and the birds in the sky and over every living creature that moves on the ground (Gen. 1:28).

MANY people make new resolutions only at the beginning of the year. But every new day is a time to start and a fresh opportunity for a happy new beginning! Begin every new day with determination. With God's love and through His grace, you have the ability to move into the season of the miraculous and toward your destiny.

Therefore, this is the time to subdue and take dominion over every act of rebellion (see Gen. 1:28). This is when you can recover all you have lost in the past (see 1 Sam. 30:8). And also to take dominance in the marketplace (see 2 Kings 4:7).

This is your eleventh hour into victory. The God of honor shall visit you. May the Lord send blessing on your barns and on everything you put to hand to do! May you know the power of His resurrection in all that concerns you!

Your life will not be the same—it will be changed for good!

**Are you excited or frightened about
starting your new day?**

His Glory

He received honor and glory from God the Father when the voice came to him from the Majestic Glory, saying, "This is my Son, whom I love; with him I am well pleased"
(2 Peter 1:17).

GLORY is the outward appearances of the attributes and nature of God. Moses said to God, *"show me Your glory"* (Exod. 33:18), and God displayed His majesty, awesomeness, compassion, mercy, and His protection.

Jesus received honor and glory from God—and you have received the same as you are a child of your heavenly Father.

Expect eternal weight of glory to be released upon you and surely the King of glory will Himself tabernacle with you! Your expectation shall not be cut short!

Would you be as bold as Moses to ask God to see His glory?

Humility and Greatness

Therefore God exalted him to the highest place and gave him the name that is above every name, that at the name of Jesus every knee should bow, in heaven and on earth and under the earth, and every tongue acknowledge that Jesus Christ is Lord, to the glory of God the Father (Philippians 2:9-11).

M AY this passage be realized in your life today and forevermore! Jesus submitted to God even to the point of death on the cross. He died and was buried, but He was resurrected. Paradoxically, sometimes the way up means first going down in humility.

May you know the power inherent in humility and may the spirit of obedience take you to your highest in God.

Are humbling experiences hard to accept?

Let the Peace of God Rule

May the God of hope fill you with all joy and peace as you trust in him, so that you may overflow with hope by the power of the Holy Spirit (Romans 15:13).

THE measure of peace you enjoy determines your height in your walk with God. True peace is a gift from God.

With joy you can draw water from the well of salvation (see Isa. 2:3). Your miracle is nearer than you think! The Kingdom of God is righteousness, peace, and joy in the Holy Spirit (see Rom. 14:17).

You have to make a serious effort to readjust every inharmonious circumstance in your life to align with the original purpose of God. This requires a time of prayers and consecration in joyful expectation.

May you always be joyful in God.

Are you peaceful and joyful?

The Blood of Jesus

For you know that it was not with perishable things such as silver or gold that you were redeemed from the empty way of life handed down to you from your ancestors, but with the precious blood of Christ, a lamb without blemish or defect (1 Peter 1:18-19).

THE blood of the Lamb of God not only takes away the sins of the world, it is the most powerful force in the universe. The power of the lion of the tribe of Judah is in the blood of the Lamb who was slain.

For more than 2,000 years ago until today, the blood of Jesus is still redeeming people, bringing healing, speaking eternal things, and washing us whiter than snow!

Come expecting that this sacred ordinance instituted by our Lord will do for you all He intended it to do for you!

There is power in the blood! Always plead the blood of Lamb into all your situations.

Do you need to be washed with the blood of the Lamb?

Help from the Rock of Ages

As I looked, thrones were set in place, and the Ancient of Days took his seat. His clothing was as white as snow; the hair of his head was white like wool. His throne was flaming with fire, and its wheels were all ablaze (Daniel 7:9).

THE prophet Daniel had a dream in which he saw the assembly of the court of God and he saw the Ancient of Days (the Rock of Ages) take His seat on His throne of judgement (see Dan. 7:8-12).

The only source of complete and peaceful restoration comes from the Rock of Ages. *"Refrain your voice from weeping, and your eyes from tears; for your work shall be rewarded, says the LORD, and they shall come back from the land of the enemy. There is hope in your future, says the LORD"* (Jer. 31:16-17 NKJV).

He who promises is faithful to bring it to pass. Just as Daniel saw justice brought to injustice, may God also bring justice to every injustice in your life and bloodline.

How secure would you feel hiding in the cleft of the Rock of Ages?

A Personal Prophecy Response

Timothy, my son, I am giving you this command in keeping with the prophecies once made about you, so that by recalling them you may fight the battle well, holding on to faith and a good conscience, which some have rejected and so have suffered shipwreck with regard to the faith (1 Timothy 1:18-19).

IT is essential that you learn how to respond to a personal prophecy and understand dreams. Always keep things simple, have a positive mind, be humble realizing often these promises are possibilities that require your cooperation to actualize in the natural life!

Four keys are worthy of note in this regard: 1) fight with your personal prophesies, that is challenge your situation with what God has said to you and do not allow the situation to bring doubts to your mind; 2) hold on to faith because without faith, it is impossible to please God; 3) keep a clear conscience, putting God first in everything; 4) do not reject prophecies as some have done, which results in shipwrecks.

Have you been shipwrecked lately?

Proclamation and Decrees

*Behold I have put My words in your mouth. See, I have
this day set you over the nations* [challenges] *and over the
kingdoms* [rulers of darkness], *to root out and pull down, to
destroy and throw down, to build and to plant*
(Jeremiah 1:9-10 NKJV).

E VERY opportunity in His gracious presence is a time for prayers
as well as a time for proclamations and decrees to be established!

God wants to renew and reissue His truth and power in your life!
The mouth is an instrument of warfare in the hands of God if used
correctly, and detrimental if used in the hands of the devil.

For your proclamation and decrees to be powerful, remember,
the power of the words of your mouth, among other factors, depends
on your spiritual standing with God, your legitimate right over the
issue, and how it lines up with God's plans.

**Do the words of your mouth reflect
the love of your heavenly Father?**

Facilitating Heaven on Earth

*And you, child, will be called the prophet of the Highest; for you will go before the face of the Lord to prepare His ways, to give knowledge of salvation to His people by the remission of their sin. through the tender mercy of our God, with which the Dayspring from on high has visited us; to give light to those who sit in darkness and the shadow of death, to guide our feet into the way of peace. So the child grew and became strong in spirit, and was in the deserts till **the day of his manifestation** to Israel* (Luke 1:76-80 NKJV).

P RAYERS and fasting facilitate the agenda of heaven on earth! We move toward a day called "the day of your manifestation."

You, too, will start manifesting your destiny on earth.

**What does this Scripture passage from
Luke 1 mean to you?**

Pray and Cease Not

*For this reason we also, since the day we heard it, do not **cease** to **pray** for you, and to ask that you may be filled with the knowledge of His will in all wisdom and spiritual understanding* (Colossians 1:9 NKJV).

Y ou need to pray always, for others and yourself, so in your hunger God will give you bread of Heaven; in your thirst, water from the Rock—and for your future, land to possess, as He did for the Israelites:

In their hunger you gave them bread from heaven and in their thirst you brought them water from the rock; you told them to go in and take possession of the land you had sworn with uplifted hand to give them (Nehemiah 9:15).

On this day, God will turn the table on your enemies who have hoped to overpower you and give you the upper hand.

**Knowing that you have the upper hand today,
what will you do differently?**

Righteousness and Kindness

*It is because of him that you are in Christ Jesus, who has become for us wisdom from God—that is, our **righteousness**, holiness and redemption* (1 Corinthians 1:30).

G OD is always moved by acts of righteousness and kindness. That is why Jacob was able to say, *"So my righteousness will answer for me in time to come"* (Gen. 30:33); like Jacob, your time has come, and He and your good deeds will answer for you also!

Don't be weary in well-doing, for in due season you will reap your reward! Therefore never be weary in doing what is righteous.

*Flee the evil desires of youth and pursue **righteousness**, faith, love and peace, along with those who call on the Lord out of a pure heart* (2 Timothy 2:22).

*Consider therefore the **kindness** and sternness of God: sternness to those who fell, but **kindness** to you, provided that you continue in his **kindness**. Otherwise, you also will be cut off* (Romans 11:22).

Are you as kind and righteous as you should be?

The Fruits of Righteousness

THE Book of Leviticus is often difficult and boring to read, but it also contains some great blessings of the Bible. Here are some of these blessings:

*If you follow my decrees and are careful to obey my commands, I will send you **rain** in its season, and the ground will yield its **crops** and the trees their **fruit**. Your threshing will continue until grape harvest and the grape harvest will continue until planting, and you will eat all the **food** you want and live in **safety** in your land. I will grant **peace** in the land, and you will lie down and no one will make you afraid. I will **remove wild beasts** from the land, and the sword will not pass through your country. You will pursue your enemies, and they will fall by the sword before you. Five of you will chase a hundred, and a hundred of you will chase ten thousand, and your **enemies will fall** by the sword before you. I will look on you with favor and make you **fruitful** and **increase your numbers,** and I **will keep my covenant** with you. You will still be eating last year's harvest when you will have to move it out to make room for the new. I will put **my dwelling place among you**, and I will not abhor you. **I will walk among you** and be your God, and you will be my people. I am the LORD your God, who brought you out of Egypt so that you would no longer be slaves to the Egyptians; I broke the bars of your yoke and enabled you to **walk with heads held high** (Leviticus 26:3-13).*

Blessings are waiting for you if you obey His commands. Are you ready to receive?

Rainy Season Blessings

In the Leviticus passage from yesterday, these blessings are awaiting you:

- your ground will yield its crops
- trees of the field their fruits
- threshing season into the harvest
- harvest season into the planting
- you will eat food to the full
- you will live in safety without fear
- God will remove savage beasts from your land
- enemies will not overrun you
- you pursue and defeat your enemies
- God will show you favor
- God will make you fruitful
- He will increase your number
- He will keep His covenant with you
- you will be eating the old when the new comes in
- God will dwell among you
- God will break the bands of the yokes of your oppression

You will walk with your head held high
Do these blessings appeal to you?

The Anointing

Say to the Israelites, 'This is to be my sacred anointing oil for the generations to come (Exodus 30:31).

Anointing is the powerful expression of the Holy Spirit and has many characteristics including:

1. Fresh anointing gives the light of God. *"Command the Israelites to bring you clear* [fresh/pure] *oil of pressed olives for the light so that the lamps may be kept burning continually"* (Lev. 24:2). So let your light so shine as you live in the light of God.

2. Anointing is subject to renewal. *"The lamps on the pure gold lampstand before the LORD must be tended continually"* (Lev. 24:4). It is your responsibility to keep your anointing sharp and fresh. The choice is yours.

3. The anointing is not constant in intensity; for example, Elisha asked for music to enhance his prophetic anointing. The anointing fluctuates, diminishes, or increases depending on what you do or don't do. And even more importantly, these things can happen without the person realizing it. For example, Samson woke and he did not have the anointing. Do not move in presumption; make sure your anointing is fresh and full.

May your oil never run dry, and may your water never cease to flow.

Are you fresh and full of anointing?

His Ways Made Known

If You are pleased with me, teach me Your ways so I may know You and continue to find favor with You... (Exodus 33:13).

THE psalmist wrote, "He made known His ways to Moses" (Ps. 103:7). Moses is the one in Exodus (see above) who asked God to show him His ways.

The lessons:

- If the Lord is pleased with you, He will teach you His ways.

- You need to ask God to teach you His ways: Prayers! Prayers! Pray without ceasing.

- Only by learning His ways can you have true knowledge of Him. It is by revelation that we know God.

- Continue in His ways and His presence to find His favor.

Remember, this is your year of favor upon favor
and upon favor upon your life.
How eager are you to learn His ways?

When the Lord Touches Your Heart

*Saul also went to his home in Gibeah, accompanied by valiant men whose **hearts God had touched*** (1 Samuel 10:26).

WE all need the Lord to touch our hearts that we may do His will and also touch the hearts of others before they are drawn to us! This is crucial in this world tending to absolute humanism.

When the Lord appoints, He provides; when He sends, He supplies the necessities; and when He commissions a task, He touches the hearts of the people to work it out!

There is a river whose streams make glad the city of God, the holy place where the Most High dwells. God is within her, she will not fall; God will help her at break of day (Psalm 46:4-5).

Indeed, the Lord will help you at the break of day—and all throughout the days, weeks, months, and years.

**What do you enjoy most when
the Lord touches your heart?**

Divine Panic in the Enemies Camp

Then panic struck the whole army—those in the camp and field, and those in the outposts and raiding parties—and the ground shook. It was a panic sent by God (1 Samuel 14:15).

THERE are different types of weapons in the arsenal of God, even the wicked is a weapon for God to use to obtain His purpose!

Once God used a lying spirit to lure King Ahab to death. God can use panic and confusion as instruments of warfare. Know for sure as you pray that God can send panic and confusion to the camp of your enemies:

> *In that first attack Jonathan and his armor-bearer killed some twenty men in an area of about half an acre. Then panic struck the whole army—those in the camp and field, and those in the outposts and raiding parties—and the ground shook.* **It was a panic sent by God.** *Saul's lookouts at Gibeah in Benjamin saw the army melting away in all directions"* (1 Samuel 14:14-16.)

It is important that you realize that prayers count, and you are making a great difference as you help implement the agenda of Heaven on earth.

Has the Lord given the devil a panic attack on your account?

God will Destroy the Spoiler in Your Life

My angel will go ahead of you and bring you into the land...
(Exodus 23:23).

THE spoiler is anything that comes to bring disappointment at the verge of your breakthrough! This is what Prophet Isaiah said:

The nations shall rush like the rushing of many waters: but God shall rebuke them, and they shall flee far off, and shall be chased as the chaff of the mountains before the wind, and like a rolling thing before the whirlwind. And behold at evening-tide trouble; and before the morning he is not. **This is the portion of them that spoil us, and the lot of them that rob us**" (Isaiah 17:13-14 KJV).

Even as the Lord sends His angels ahead of us to bring us to the place He has prepared (see Exod. 23:20), God will cut off *"the Amorites, the Jebusites, the Hittites, the Perizzites, Canaanights and the Hivites"* from our Promised Land (see Exod. 23:23). Whatever these names symbolize in your life, God will cut them off.

As the spoiler in your life is cast out, God will send His presence to you with manifested mercy, compassion, grace, power, and favor (see Exod. 33:12-19). And the Lord will hold your right hand and empower it for His purpose.

Have you allowed the Lord to cast out the spoiler(s) in your life?

Reading the Bible in a Year: Deuteronomy 31-32 & Luke 1:1-23.

Build an Altar for God

Make an altar of earth for Me and sacrifice on it your burnt offerings and fellowship offering, your sheep, and your goats and your cattle. Wherever I cause my name to be honored, I will come to you and bless you (Exodus 20:24).

AN altar is a place of meeting between you and God; a place of sacrifice; a place of worship; a place where His name is honored; a place of divine exchange; your place of prayers.

Note: God does not want a fanciful place, but a place as natural and ordinary as possible. The Bible tells us that in ancient times people built altars to God as memorials.

If you don't have one, will you build Him an altar today in your bedroom, sitting room, or prayer closet? He promised to come to you there and bless you.

Have you built God an altar?

Double Open Doors Before You

*Thus says the Lord to His anointed; to Cyrus, whose right hand I have held [empowered] to subdue nations before him and loose the armor of kings, **to open before him the double doors**...I will give you the treasures of darkness and hidden riches of secret places...* (Isaiah 45:1-3 NKJV).

GOD is the One who opens doors for you with empowerment. If He opens a double door, He will doubly empower. This is what He said to Cyrus. Before opening the double doors for Cyrus, God anointed him, held his right hand, and subdued kings before him!

May the Lord empower your right hand and give you keys to take the treasures of darkness.

Do you allow God to hold your right hand?

Don't Use Human Plans and Methods

*It is true that I am an ordinary, weak human being, but **I don't use human plans and methods to win my battles**. I use God's mighty weapons, not those made by men, to knock down the devil's strongholds. These weapons can break down every proud argument against God and every wall that can be built to keep men from finding Him* (2 Corinthians 10:3-5 Living Bible).

THERE are many all-time classic statements accredited to Apostle Paul, but this one stands out as worthy of daily remembrance (see above).

Indeed, the weapons of our warfare are not carnal, because our battles and our enemies are not always carnal—they are spiritual.

For we do not wrestle against flesh and blood, but against principalities, against powers, against the rulers of the darkness of this age, against spiritual hosts of wickedness in the heavenly places (Ephesians 6:12 NKJV).

Your victory is secured in Christ! Knock down every evil plan that stands against you and your family.

Are you equipped for spiritual warfare?

Mount Sinai— God's Holy Mountain

Now Mount Sinai was completely in smoke, because the LORD descended upon it in fire. Its smoke ascended like the smoke of a furnace, and the whole mountain quaked greatly (Exodus 18:19 NKJV).

O f all the mountains in the world, why is Mount Sinai called God's Holy Mountain?

This mountain is known for many outstanding occurrences. Most of all, this mountain is revered for the powerful manifestation of the holiness of God. Holiness, therefore, has power and holiness speaks loudly sometimes! *"When the people saw the thunder and lightning and heard the trumpet and saw the mountain in smoke, they trembled with fear. ...Do not have God speak to us or we will die"* (Exod. 20:18-19).

This was the unveiled presence of God! So awesome! So great was the reverent fear that the people stayed at a distance from the mountain. How mighty were His signs and wonders displayed!

That same presence lives in you, but now it is veiled so that you are not consumed. Same power; same might—in you! You are a walking terror to the devil and his evil ones! Today, march on as His weapon of war—God's battleaxe—as you prepare to gain what rightly belongs to you.

What do you think about being a walking terror to the evil ones?

Your Strength Is in
Your Identity in Christ

*I have been **crucified** with **Christ** and I no longer live, but **Christ** lives in me. The life I now live in the body, I live by faith in the Son of God, who loved me and gave himself for me* (Galatians 2:20).

IF I had the choice of saying how I would like to be best known, I would choose to be known in Christ and Him crucified!

If my enemies are to fear me, let them fear me because I am in Him and He is in me. This was how Mordecai's enemies referred to him. *"But Haman...told Zeresh his wife and all his friends everything that had befallen him. Then said his wise men and Zeresh his wife unto him if Mordecai be of the **seed of the Jews,** before whom thou hast begun to fall, thou shalt not prevail against him, but shalt surely fall before him"* (Esther 6:12-13 KJV).

In the same way, because you are of the seed of Christ, your adversary shall fall before you! Yes, greater is Christ in you than the devil in the world. Be assured you are never alone! Be bold, the righteous are as bold as a lion.

Are you emboldened knowing that you are the seed of Christ and never alone?

The Waters of Marah and Elim

Moses led Israel from the Red Sea on to the Wilderness of Shur. They traveled for three days through the wilderness without finding any water. They got to Marah, but they couldn't drink the water at Marah; it was bitter. That's why they called the place Marah (Bitter). And the people complained to Moses, "So what are we supposed to drink?" So Moses cried out in prayer to God. God pointed him to a stick of wood. Moses threw it into the water and the water turned sweet (Exodus 15:22-25 Message Bible).

THERE is always a sign from God that He is with you, no matter how tough the situation may seem. His help is always around the corner. For the Israelites in the midst of their desert journey, on their way to the Promised Land, a land flowing with milk and honey, they encountered untold hardship.

But God brought them to a place of temporary refuge and comfort! God brought them to Elim—a place of twelve streams and seventy palm trees (see Exod. 15:27). Elim was a welcome relief from the barrenness and bitterness of the wasteland of Shur.

May the God of the Hebrews deliver you from all wastelands, turn any bitterness to sweetness, and bring you to your Elim—rest and blessings—as you enter into your Promised Land.

Are you ready for some rest and blessings?

There Are More with Us

One night the Lord spoke to Paul in a vision "Don't be afraid;
keep on speaking, do not be silent. For I am with you, and no
one is going to attack and harm you, because I have many
people in this city" (Acts 18:9-10).

How easy it is for us to forget that we are part of God's army, that we have other innumerable soldiers of the Lord, visible and invisible, active and reserved, all about us. I pray that this fact will testify in every area of your life! God has many people surrounding you, protecting you, loving you. Trust Him.

If God be for you, nobody can be against you. You are covered by the blood of Jesus. Be bold and courageous! You shall not fail.

Have you identified those around you
who are on God's side?

Encourage Yourself

But those who wait for the Lord [who expect, look for, and hope in Him] shall change and renew their strength and power; they shall lift their wings and mount up [close to God] as eagles [mount up to the sun]; they shall run and not be weary, they shall walk and not faint or become tired (Isaiah 40:31 AMP).

THIS passage from Isaiah (see above) clearly teaches us to know the benefits of waiting on God. Further, it explains how to wait on Him; let our expectations be based on Christ, let us look up to Him, the Author and Finisher of our faith; let our hope be anchored on HIM who alone is able to stop us from falling.

If you wait the proper way, you will experience transformation and increase of His power in your life; move into closer intimacy with God; soar like an eagle mounted up to the sun.

And He will be God of all seasons for you; whether you are in the waiting, walking, or running season, you will not be weary or tired.

**Have you learned how to be your
own best encourager?**

Light will Break Forth Quickly

*Your light will break forth like the dawn, and your healing
will quickly appear; then your righteousness will go before
you, and the glory of the Lord will be your rear guard"*
(Isaiah 58:8)

EVERYWHERE there is darkness means the absence of light. God
is the Father of light and in Him there is no darkness at all. His
Kingdom is the Kingdom of marvelous light, and the devil's kingdom
is the kingdom of darkness.

When the Bible says that light will break forth and your healing will appear, it means, among other things, that His Kingdom is
coming into your life. When His Kingdom comes, He will grant you
victory over every injustice.

In His Kingdom, God will meet your needs *"according to His
riches in glory by Christ Jesus"* (Phil. 4:19). With the breaking forth
of light comes divine deliverance, wisdom, and abundance of revelations from His throne.

Have you seen the Light?
Have you been granted victory?

I Wish You a Three-Year Harvest

Follow my decrees and be careful to obey my laws. ...Then the land will yield its fruit, and you will eat your fill and live there in safety. You may ask, "What will we eat in the seventh year if we do not plant or harvest our crops?" I will send you such a blessing in the sixth year that the land will yield enough for three years (Leviticus 25:18-21).

IMAGINE three years of interrupted blessings. This is how the Bible puts one such outpouring from God.

Note that there will be enough provisions for the:

- Sixth year—the year of your blessing.
- Seventh year—the year of rest, the year of no hard labor, no toil.
- Eighth year—and the year after until harvest.

We serve a perfect God! He has all things on hand for our benefit! This is a continuous process, when you get to the eighth year, the sixth year will begin again.

Are you ready for three years of interrupted blessings?

Test Yourself

Check up on yourselves. Are you really Christians? Do you feel Christ's presence and power more and more within you? Or are you just pretending to be Christians when actually you aren't at all? (2 Corinthians 13:5-6 Living Bible).

MAY you always walk in His power! To enjoy His power within you, you need to be continuously immersed in the blood of Jesus. Do you know Him and the power of His might? More than ever before, the need to remind yourself of this is growing each day.

Many a Christian seems to so easily forget the power of God that is at work in them and rather focus on the magnitude of the devil's challenges and intrigues against them.

As Paul prayed for the Ephesians, that is how I stand for you!

*I have not stopped giving thanks for you, remembering you in my prayers. I keep asking that the God of our Lord Jesus Christ, the glorious Father, may give you the Spirit of wisdom and revelation, so that you may know him better. I pray that the eyes of your heart may be enlightened in order that you may know the hope to which he has called you, the riches of his glorious inheritance in his holy people, and his incomparably **great power for us** who believe. **That power is the same as the mighty strength** (Ephesians 1:16-19).*

Have you been focusing on His power within you or the devil's snares?

Power to You

*For **the Spirit God** gave us does not make us timid, but **gives
us power**, love and self-discipline* (2 Timothy 1:7).

You tap into the power of God in your life when you reach out to others with the gospel as the Bible instructs to do. This is what happened when the disciples went on an outreach, *"After this the Lord appointed seventy-two others and sent them two by two ahead of him to every town and place where he was about to go. The seventy-two returned with joy and said, "Lord, even the demons submit to us in your name"* (Luke 10:1,17).

In this passage, God's power became manifest only when they went out! But the truth is that they had the power all the time. Obey Him and you will connect with the supernaturalness of the infinite God.

Even the thorn in your flesh should not stop you!

**What steps can you take today to release
the power within for His glory?**

Don't Let a Thorn Stop You

And lest I should be exalted above measure through the abundance of the revelations, there was given to me a thorn in the flesh, the messenger of Satan to buffet me, lest I should be exalted above measure (2 Corinthians 12:7 KJV).

I do not know what Apostle Paul's thorn in the flesh was, but whatever might be the thorn in your own flesh, do not let it stop you from pursuing your goals in life. Everyone has a thorn in their flesh!

even though I have received such wonderful revelations from God. So to keep me from becoming proud, I was given a thorn in my flesh, a messenger from Satan to torment me and keep me from becoming proud (2 Corinthians 12:7 NLT).

For most people, the thorn in the flesh is meant to keep them in a place of humility that God might exalt them!

**What is the thorn in your flesh?
Is it holding you back?**

God Makes All Grace Abound to You

And God is able to make all grace abound toward you, that you, always having all sufficiency in all things, may have an abundance for every good work (2 Corinthians 9:8 NKJV).

GRACE is the unmerited favor of God in our lives but it is in practical reality, the power of God working through humankind. The Bible says *"God is able to make all grace abound toward you."* This is true, don't let the issues of life deny you of this eternal truth; let it testify in your life.

Make conscious efforts to allow room for God's grace in your life. God never fails!

How do you specifically identify God's grace?

God Speaks from a Place of Mercy

*But **in your great mercy** you did not put an end to them or abandon them, for **you are a gracious and merciful God*** (Nehemiah 9:31).

THE mercy of God is His grace to us that exempts us from judgment. God instructed Moses to construct the ark of covenant with a mercy seat between two cherubim. This is so that He will meet and speak to Moses from a place of mercy.

Imagine this: God wants to speak to us from a place of mercy. *"When Moses entered the Tent of Meeting to speak with the LORD, he heard the voice speaking to him from between the two cherubim above the atonement cover on the ark of the covenant law. In this way the LORD spoke to him"* (Numbers 7:89).

In their most trying times, God spoke to the Israelites from a place of mercy, which was also to them a place of sacrifice, a place of power, and of testimony. The cherubim represent or symbolize God's supernatural nature and His divine help that is always available to us. The seat of atonement is the constant reminder of His supreme sacrifice for us when we were yet sinners.

May He remember you in His mercy.

How do you specifically identify God's mercy?

The Prayers God Answers

Jabez cried out to the God of Israel, "Oh, that you would bless me and enlarge my territory! Let your hand be with me, and keep me from harm so that I will be free from pain." And God granted his request (1 Chronicles 4:10).

THIS was the prayer of Jabez. Jabez confronted his situation without blame shifting and confessed the truth of the situation. He did not blame his mother for giving him such name but instead invited in the hands of God.

His prayer was selfless and broadly along the following lines: He prayed that God would prosper him in the fullness of God's power. He prayed that God would enlarge his territory. He asked that God's hand would be with him. And he prayed that he would no longer be in pain or be a cause of pain to others.

These are the prayers that God answers.

Are you praying along those same lines?

Overcoming Intrigues

In the shelter of your presence you hide them, from the intrigues of men, in your dwelling you keep them safe from accusing tongues (Psalm 31:20).

THE intrigues of humankind are varied as we live in this world. Intrigues try to influence your fleshy nature—the Jacob in you—and corrupt your spiritual being—the Israel in you.

Now the works of the flesh are evident, which are: adultery, fornication, uncleanness, lewdness, idolatry, sorcery, hatred, contentions, jealousies, outbursts of wrath, selfish ambitions, dissensions, heresies, envy, murders, drunkenness, revelries, and the like; of which I tell you beforehand, just as I also told you in time past, that those who practice such things will not inherit the kingdom of God (Galatians 5:19-21 NKJV).

But God says He will defeat the plans of evil against you and that you will become His showcase children.

**Have intrigues been keeping you
from seeking God's face?**

God Turns Curses into Blessings

"It may be that the LORD will look upon my misery and restore to me his covenant blessing instead of his curse today." So David and his men continued along the road while Shimei was going along the hillside opposite him, cursing as he went and throwing stones at him and showering him with dirt (2 Samuel 16:12-13).

THERE is an hour that is called "the hour that Shimei reigns." This is the time when you allow insults and humiliation from a weaker source to go by without being too unduly concerned. Sometimes it is God-ordained to humble you. If you can hold yourself in control, God will always avenge the hour the Shimei reigned.

Shiemei's reign is the time or season in our lives when the situation allows shame, challenges, and insults from the enemy to provoke you to ungodly reaction. But it is God who avenges in this hour! For King David, God turned the cursing of Shimei into an opportunity to bless him.

Are you easily provoked when insulted or humiliated?

Blessings and Rewards of Obedience

If you fully obey the LORD your God and carefully follow all his commands I give you today, the LORD your God will set you high above all the nations on earth (Deuteronomy 28:1).

BLESSING is the power of God that enables us to perform—and divine enablement. Obedience is living and carrying out God's commandments. Blessing and obedience are interconnected. They both produce fruits in your life. See Leviticus 26:3-13.

The following Scripture passages are proof of God's promise that if you obey Him, your life will be blessed:

- and through your offspring all nations on earth will be blessed, because you have **obey**ed me (Gen. 22:18).
- Now if you **obey** me fully and keep my covenant, then out of all nations you will be my treasured possession (Exod. 19:5).
- Follow my decrees and be careful to **obey** my laws, and you will live safely in the land (Lev. 25:18).
- the terms I commanded your ancestors when I brought them out of Egypt, out of the iron-smelting furnace.' I said, '**Obey** me and do everything I command you, and you will be my people, and I will be your God (Jer. 11:14).
- But if anyone **obey**s his word, love for God is truly made complete in them. This is how we know we are in him (1 John 2:5).

Can you think of other passages that confirm His promise of blessings?

Patient Endurance

Whether the cloud stayed over the tabernacle for two days or a month or a year, the Israelites would remain in camp and not set out; but when it lifted, they would set out. At the LORD's command they encamped, and at the LORD's command they set out. They obeyed the LORD's order, in accordance with his command through Moses (Numbers 9:22-23).

PATIENTLY, they waited, whether for two days or a year, because they were focused on the cloud of glory. The Israelites obeyed the command given to them through Moses; the natural circumstance did not determine their actions; they acted as directed by God.

God uses people to achieve His goals. This is the essence of patient endurance. Being patient and enduring uncomfortable circumstances goes against most people's nature. This is something that believers must work on to become a good and faithful servant of the Lord.

How patient are you?

Let God Arise—
His Enemy Scattered

Whenever the ark set out, Moses said, "Rise up, O LORD! May your enemies be scattered; may your foes flee before you." Whenever it came to rest, he said, "Return, O LORD, to the countless thousands of Israel" (Numbers 10:35-36).

THIS verse in Numbers reminds us of the kindness and serenity of God's presence. God's enemies are scattered when He arises, and when He rests, His kindness and glory abides in Israel.

This is likewise with you—He desires to surround you with His presence, which brings kindness and serenity. He also desires to scatter your enemies.

Whatever areas you have not felt the presence and power of God in your life, may God arise and make Himself known to you. Know that your enemies will scatter before you when He is present.

**Do you have enemies
you would like to see scattered?**

Beware of the Mixed Multitude Influence

Now the mixed multitude who were among them yielded to intense craving; so the children of Israel also wept again and said: "Who will give us meat to eat?" (Numbers 11:4)

THE *mixed multitude* may symbolically represent areas in your life that have not yet taken on Christlikeness, weakness, or the unholy influence of others. Every person is a bag of flesh pitted against the spirit. Flesh tries to resurrect, but we must kill it each time.

The power of flesh that is not crucified will always rise up as challenges during our journey. If we cannot crucify these desires of the flesh or aliens among us, they will continue to influence and try to hijack your destiny.

Are you being influenced by a mixed multitude?
What can you do to stop the assault?

Develop Your Gifts

The manna was like coriander seed and looked like resin.
The people went around gathering it, and then ground it
in a hand mill or crushed it in a mortar. They cooked it in
a pot or made it into loaves. And it tasted like something
made with olive oil (Numbers 11:7-8).

O UR gifts are like the manna the Israelites had in their wilderness
It is our responsibility to develop them into what we want them
to be. We need to gather (discover or identify) it, ground (master
understand, be knowledgeable in its operations) it, or crush (sum-
mit it to God, walk in humility, or ensure it is used for other people's
benefit) it in a mortar.

This is what counts and it makes a significant difference in the
Kingdom of God. God gave you specific gifts that will enhance and
enlarge His Kingdom.

Are you using your gifts to His glory?

Do Not be Afraid

*The land we passed through and explored is exceedingly good. If the Lord is pleased with us, He will lead us into that land, a land flowing with milk and honey, and will give it to us. Only **do not rebel against the Lord**. And **do not be afraid** of the people of the land, because we will swallow them up. Their protection is gone, but **the Lord is with us.** Do not be afraid of them* (Numbers 14:7-9).

THE passage from Numbers 14 is the voice of faith, wisdom, and trust that came through the mouth of men with excellent spirits—Caleb and Joshua—after their spy mission to the Promised Land.

This spirit can be true of you today as it was true to the people of Israel in the time of Joshua and Caleb. "Do not be afraid," is an admonishment to you as you walk through each day that can be full of unknowns. God is known—and He loves you dearly.

Meditate on that!

What are you afraid of?

You are the Epaphras of Our Time

Epaphras, who is one of yourselves, a servant of Christ Jesus, sends you [saints of God] greetings. [He is] always striving for you [saints] earnestly in his prayers, [pleading] that you may [as persons of ripe character and clear conviction] stand firm and mature [in spiritual growth], convinced and fully assured in everything willed by God (Colossians 4:12 AMP).

I call you Epaphras because I believe you are the Epaphras of our time! I believe you are also praying for others and standing firm. I believe you are maturing in your faith and are confident in God's will as you lift up others before your heavenly Father.

Now He who searches the hearts knows what the mind of the Spirit is, because He makes intercession for the saints according to the will of God (Romans 8:27).

What an awesome commitment to see others fulfill their purpose in God! As you do this, your labor of love will not go unrewarded!

Are you earnestly praying for others like Epaphras?

Your Privilege

*Acknowledge that **the Lord is God**! He made us, and we are his. We are his people, the sheep of his pasture. Enter his gates with thanksgiving; go into his courts with praise. Give thanks to him and praise his name. For the Lord is good. His unfailing love continues forever, and his faithfulness continues to each generation* (Psalm 100:3-5 NLT).

In the words of Moses, *"Acknowledge and take to heart this day that **the Lord is God** in heaven above and on the earth below. There is no other"* (Deut. 4:39).

You have a unique privilege—to know God, the Creator of Heaven and earth, on a personal and intimate level. Whatever may come across your path in life, prevail over it with this realization!

Indeed, He made us, we are His people, the sheep of His pasture! If God be for you, who can be against you; you will not fail.

I am praying for you.

Do you daily acknowledge that the Lord is God?

Your Breakthrough

So there at Hebron, King David made a covenant before the Lord with all the elders of Israel. And they anointed him king of Israel. David was thirty years old when he began to reign, and he reigned forty years in all. He had reigned over Judah from Hebron for seven years and six months, and from Jerusalem he reigned over all Israel and Judah for thirty-three years (2 Samuel 5:3-5 NLT).

THERE is the place of your breakthrough, the place of unity, anointing, and intimate fellowship with God. The Bible describes a place in the history of the Hebrews where these things happened, and the place is called Hebron.

Are you praying for a breakthrough in your career, finances, marriage, health, or relationships with your children or parents? You shall without fail enter the Hebron of your life!

I pray that whatever you are facing, God will bring you to your Hebron.

Are you believing for your breakthrough in prayer?

Reading the Bible in a Year: 1 Samuel 15-16 & Luke 14:25-35.

Be Encouraged!

*From the time he put him in charge of his household and of all that he owned, **the LORD blessed the household of the Egyptian because of Joseph.** The **blessing of the LORD** was on everything Potiphar had, both in the house and in the field* (Genesis 39:5).

T HERE are four blessings that are yours to accept. Two are shared today and two more tomorrow.

1. Like Joseph, whatever the enemy has done to you will turn out for your good. *"Say to him, 'Be careful, keep calm and don't be afraid. Do not lose heart because of these two smoldering stubs of firewood—because of the fierce anger of Rezin and Aram and of the son of Remaliah. Aram, Ephraim and Remaliah's son have plotted your ruin, saying, "Let us invade Judah; let us tear it apart and divide it among ourselves, and make the son of Tabeel king over it." Yet this is what the Sovereign LORD says: "It will not take place, it will not happen"* (Isa. 7:4-7).

2. As Joseph was eventually vindicated, you will be vindicated, so look up to the arm of God and not to the arm of flesh. *"Be strong and courageous. Do not be afraid or discouraged because of the king of Assyria and the vast army with him, for there is a greater power with us than with him. With him is an arm of flesh; but with us is the Lord our God, to help us and to fight our battles" And the people were strengthened by the words of Hezekiah king of Judah"* (2 Chronicles 32:7-8).

Have you accepted these blessings with thanksgiving?

Be Encouraged Again!

3. Joseph held on to his righteousness, you too will hold on to righteousness and your righteousness will bear fruits. *"You heavens above, rain down my righteousness; let the clouds shower it down. Let the earth open wide, let salvation spring up, let righteousness flourish with it; I, the LORD, have created it"* (Isa. 45:8).

4. Like Joseph, the purpose of God in your life will be fulfilled and glory and excellency shall be restored to you. *"The desert and the parched land will be glad; the wilderness will rejoice and blossom. Like the crocus, it will burst into bloom; it will rejoice greatly and shout for joy. The glory of Lebanon will be given to it, the splendor of Carmel and Sharon they will see the glory of the LORD, the splendor of our God. Strengthen the feeble hands, steady the knees that give way; say to those with fearful hearts, "Be strong, do not fear; your God will come, he will come with vengeance; with divine retribution he will come to save you"* (Isa. 35:1-4).

Again, have you accepted these blessings with thanksgiving?

God Will Not Forsake You

He brought us out from there to bring us in and give us the
Land that He promised on oath to our ancestors
(Deuteronomy 6:23).

G OD brought the Israelites out of bondage and into the Promised
Land. He has promised to do the same for you. He won't bring
you out of troubles just to throw you into more. He is always with
you—protecting you and giving you strength and power to defeat
what comes against you. He did not bring you this far to fail to bring
you into His promise.

*And David said to his son Solomon, "Be strong and of **good***
courage, and do it; do not fear nor be dismayed, for the LORD
God—my God—will be with you. He will not leave you nor
forsake you" (1 Chronicles 28:20 NKJV).

He who began a good work in you will surely bring it to a perfect
conclusion!

How are you drawing on His promise to perfect you?

God Is Your Guide

Guide me in your truth and teach me, for you are God my Savior, and my hope is in you all day long (Psalm 25:5).

THIS is how Moses put it, *"surely this great nation is a wise and understanding people"* (Deut. 4:6) meaning ours is a blessed inheritance if we are guided by Him. He also said, *"What other nation is so great as to have their gods near them the way the Lord our God is near us whenever we pray to him?"* (Deut. 4:7) meaning we serve an awesome God—He guides our nation when we pray to Him. *"And what other nation is so great as to have such righteous decrees and laws as this body of laws"* (Deut. 4:8) meaning the law of the Lord is perfect, reviving the soul—they guide us into all righteousness!

Indeed! *"You, Lord, keep my lamp burning; my God turns my darkness into light. With your help I can advance against a troop; with my God I can scale a wall"* (Ps. 18:28-29).

May this be your testimony!

Have you scaled any walls lately?

A People Saved by God

Blessed are you, O Israel! Who is like you, a people saved by the Lord? He is your shield and helper and your glorious sword. Your enemies will cower before you, and you will tread on their heights (Deuteronomy 33:29).

MAY God open His fountain and pour the abundance of the richness of His promises unto you. As His children, saved by the blood of the Lamb, He is also our shield and helper and we have access to His glorious sword.

Your enemies will cower before you and you will walk before them with confidence.

*So you are no longer a slave, but **God's child;** and since **you are his child**, God has made you also **an heir*** (Galatians 4:7).

May you live with this knowledge living in your heart, mind, and spirit!

Are you prepared to receive your inheritance?

Your Past Is Not Your Future

Brothers and sisters, I do not consider myself yet to have taken hold of it. But one thing I do: Forgetting what is behind and straining toward what is ahead, I press on toward the goal to win the prize for which God has called me heavenward in Christ Jesus (Philippians 3:13-14).

Do not allow your negative past experiences to frustrate the goals ahead of you. You are what God says you are and not what your circumstances say.

Reach ahead in faith that what is in the past will serve as a catalyst to motivate you into a new and exciting future. Allow the past to serve as lessons to learn from—not hold you back. Like Paul, forget what is behind and strive for what is ahead.

Seek the prize for which God has called you heavenward in Christ Jesus.

Are you stuck in the past?

Is Your House Right with God?

If my house were not right with God, surely he would not have made with me an everlasting covenant, arranged and secured in every part; surely he would not bring to fruition my salvation and grant me my every desire (2 Samuel 23:5).

ABOVE is King David's testimony. May you enjoy the fruits of your salvation, and may His everlasting covenant rest securely on you!

This is what Joshua said of his family and you, too, can say the same of our family;

But if serving the LORD seems undesirable to you, then choose for yourselves this day whom you will serve...But as for me and my household, we will serve the LORD (Joshua 24:15).

God will stand with you as you stand with Him! As He did for David and Joshua, so He will do for you.

Is your house in order?

Reading the Bible in a Year: 2 Samuel 1-3 & Luke 18:1-17.

Divine Responsibilities

As the Lord commanded His servant Moses, so Moses commanded Joshua, and Joshua did it; he left nothing undone of all that the Lord commanded Moses (Joshua 11:15).

GOD is the God of order; and as for humankind, we are designed to need each other. The Bible passage from Joshua illustrates God divine chain of responsibility. In it you see how your seemly insignificant role is of vital necessity for the overall welfare of the corporate existence. God commanded Moses and Moses in turn commanded Joshua, and the Bible says Joshua carried it out.

There are authorities set over you who need to be treated with respect and their orders carried out. Unless they are illegal or immoral, you need to honor those in authority. God sees all, and He will honor you as you honor others—take your responsibilities seriously, God does.

Do you follow through and take responsibility?

You Are Important

Then the Lord said to Moses, "Look, I have specifically chosen Bezalel...I have filled him with the Spirit of God, giving him great wisdom, ability, and expertise in all kinds of crafts. He is a master craftsman, expert in working with gold, silver, and bronze. He is skilled in engraving and mounting gemstones and in carving wood. He is a master at every craft! ...Moreover, I have given special skill to all the gifted craftsmen so they can make all the things I have commanded you to make" (Exodus 31:1-6).

GOD showed Moses the tabernacle, but anointed others to build it. God gives each person an important role in His Kingdom.

See how God used many people to fight this battle at different fronts, *"As long as Moses held up the staff in his hand, the Israelites had the advantage. But whenever he dropped his hand, the Amalekites gained the advantage. Moses' arms soon became so tired he could no longer hold them up. So Aaron and Hur...stood on each side of Moses, holding up his hands. So his hands held steady until sunset. As a result, Joshua overwhelmed the army of Amalek in battle"* (Exod. 17:11-13).

Know today you are important—no matter your role in God's order of responsibilities.

Do you believe you are important?

The Word of God Is Life

Let the redeemed of the LORD say so, whom He has redeemed from the hand of the enemy (Psalm 107:2 NKJV).

L ET the Word of God be in your heart and in your mouth. It is the word in your mouth that speaks to your situation.

The word is near you, *"It is not up heaven so that you have to ask, 'Who will ascend into heaven to get it and proclaim it to us....' Nor is it beyond the sea so that you have to ask, 'Who will cross the sea to get it....' No, **the word is very near you**; it is **in your mouth** and in **your heart**..."* (Deut. 30:13-14).

Moses also said, *"They* [the words of God] *are not just idle words, they are your life. By them you will live long in the land..."* (Deut. 32:47). Faith is putting God's Word to work, not just waiting for God to work!

It is important that you remember to take the Word with you when you pray!

Have you been carrying the Word along with you to prayer?

Your Parents' Mistakes
Won't Hinder You

*Then they made signs to his father, to find out what he would like to name the child. He asked for a writing tablet, and to everyone's astonishment he wrote, "His name is John." Immediately his mouth was opened and his tongue set free, and he began to speak, praising God. All the neighbors were filled with awe, and throughout the hill country of Judea people were talking about all these things. Everyone who heard this wondered about it, asking, **"What then is this child going to be?"** For the Lord's hand was with him* (Luke 1:62-66).

THIS is the story about how the ministry of John the Baptist began. The father doubted the promise made by God through angel Gabriel, so he was made dumb and deaf until the naming ceremony of John when he miraculously spoke. That drew the attention of the people to John and they knew he was not an ordinary child. What a great start it was for John!

You may have had a rough childhood, many have. But may the Lord lift you up despite the circumstances of your birth, your parents, and all the circumstances that may have hindered your development.

Can you resolve today to look beyond the past and into a bright and exciting future?

Regaining a
Deserted Inheritance

Elisha died and was buried. Now Moabites raiders used to enter the country every spring. Once while some Israelites were burying a man, suddenly they saw a band of raiders; so they threw the man's body into Elisha's tomb. When the body touched Elisha's bones, the man came to life and stood up on his feet (2 Kings 13:20-21).

THE unknown man regained the deserted mantle, the inheritance. Elijah passed his mantle unto Elisha who, however, failed to pass on the mantle to another. Elisha died and was buried with all his anointing! For a while that great mantle lay wasted, buried in the ground.

Mantles are earthly bound and are not needed in Heaven. Any gifting divinely given to your ancestors that are yet lying desolate is waiting for you! If you meet the condition, you will manifest the anointing. It is possible for you to inherit all the great giftings in your ancestry with signs and wonders following!

Is there a mantel waiting for you to discover?

Nothing Missing—Fully Restored

[God said to David], *"Pursue, for you shall surely overtake them and without fail recover all. So David recovered all that the Amalekites [enemies] had carried away...And nothing of theirs was lacking, either small or great, sons or daughters, spoil or anything which they had taken from them; David recovered all* (1 Samuel 30:8,18-19 NKJV).

L IKE David, you too shall be restored—nothing will be missing, nothing broken, nothing lacking!

Moses demanded complete deliverance from the clutches of Pharaoh and from their slavery in Egypt: *"Then Pharaoh summoned Moses and said, "Go, worship the LORD. Even your women and children may go with you; only leave your flocks and herds behind. But Moses said, "You must allow us to have sacrifices and burnt offerings to present to the LORD our God. Our livestock too must go with us; not a hoof is to be left behind..."* (Exod. 10:24-26).

These are just two instances of complete deliverance and recovery!

This will be your testimony as well.

Are you listening closely for God's instruction to pursue your deliverance?

Can You Help Almighty God?

And the house of Joseph also went up against Bethel, and the LORD was with them. So the house of Joseph sent men to spy out Bethel. (The name of the city was formerly Luz.) And when the spies saw a man coming out of the city, they said to him, "Please show us the entrance to the city, and we will show you mercy." So he showed them the entrance to the city, and they struck the city with the edge of the sword; but they let the man and all his family go. And the man went to the land of the Hittites, built a city, and called its name Luz, which is its name to this day (Judges 1:22-26 NKJV).

CAN people help Almighty God? The answer is yes! The story from Judges 1 is about an unknown man who helped God.

And this is what the angel of the Lord said of the land of Meroz, who failed to help God in time of need: *"'Curse Meroz,' said the angel of the LORD, 'Curse its inhabitants bitterly, because they did not come to the help of the LORD'"* (Judg. 5:23 NKJV).

God is a rewarder, and He will reward you abundantly as you help Him; your labor of love will never go unrewarded.

In what ways can you help God today?

Crying Out to the Lord

This poor man cried out, and the Lord heard him, and saved him out of all his troubles (Psalm 34:6 NKJV).

THE Bible is clear on this—whenever God's people cry out to Him, He answers. The cry of the righteous moves God!

To Moses at the burning bush, God said, *"I have heard them **crying out** because of their slave drivers and I am concerned about their suffering. So I have come down to rescue them..."* (Exod. 3:7-8). Again and again the Israelites cried out. *"But when they **cried out** to the LORD, he raised up for them a deliverer, Othniel son of Kenaz, Caleb's younger brother, who saved them"* (Judg. 3:9). *"Again the Israelites **cried out** to the LORD, and he gave them a deliverer—Ehud..."* (Judg. 3:15). *"Because he had nine hundred chariots fitted with iron and had cruelly oppressed the Israelites for twenty years, **they cried** to the LORD for help"* (Judg. 4:3).

Each time He sent them help from His sanctuary. God is concerned about your suffering, so don't die in silence—cry out, but only to Him who is able to stop us from falling!

**Is there something keeping you from
crying out to Him?**

Do Unto Others...

...Now God has paid me back for what I did to them"
(see Judges 1:5-7).

WHAT a person sows, that is what the person reaps. Another familiar saying: What goes around comes around.

Judges tells of a story about what happens to an evildoer. Gideon caught up with two Eastern kings and asked them, *"what kind of men did you kill at Tabor?"* They said *"men like you."* So Gideon killed them saying, *"if you had spared their lives, I would not kill you"* (see Judg. 8:18-19).

Fate caught up with them. May the Lord pay back to those who have sought to spoil your destiny and all that are obstacles to the plans of God in your life!

**In what way have you noticed that
what goes around comes around?**

Preserving Core Values

*And Joseph died, all his brothers and all that generation. ...
Now there arose a new king over Egypt who **did not know**
Joseph. And he said..."Look the people of the children of Israel
are more and mightier than we; come let deal shrewdly with
them (Exodus 1:6-10a NKJV).*

T HERE came a time when the Egyptians forgot—they lost the core
values—the good that Joseph did for the land of Egypt.

Here is another story: *"After that generation* [that served the Lord
God] *died, another generation grew up, **who did not acknowledge
the Lord or remember the mighty things he had done** for Israel. The
Israelites did evil in the Lord's sight"* (Judg. 2:10-11 NLT).

It is important to set core values for our Christian lives and family based on the eternal Word of God that outlasts the generations.
Your posterity will be the better for it.

**Have you established core values in yourself,
your family?**

Inheritance for Each One

*After Joshua had dismissed the Israelites, they went to take possession of the land, each **to their own inheritance*** (Judges 2:6).

THE final outcome of your life is a factor of your personal responsibilities.

The possession of your land of promise is yours to work out or be neglected to become desolate. This is what the Bible says of the Israelites: Each person had to work on allotted inheritance.

What are you doing to possess your possessions? Each of us has allotment from Heaven. Don't waste your gifting. By taking one step at a time, you can start to work on your gifting or potential, and God will perfect it.

What steps have you taken recently to fulfill your potential?

Faith and Determination Will See You Through

When Naomi realized that Ruth was determined to go with her, she stopped urging her (Ruth 1:18).

FAITH and determination are not only infallible; they are high-water marks in the necessary prerequisites of humankind's existence. You will do well to always take them with you; they will see you through your most trying times.

Two people once faced the same challenge; one had the qualities of faith and determination (Ruth), and the other didn't (Orpah). Because of these qualities, Ruth went to the land of milk and honey, the land of God; and Orpah went back to the land of Moab, the land of wickedness and misery. The Bible says, *"Orpah kissed her mother-in-law goodbye, but Ruth **clung** to her"* (Ruth 1:14).

On the other hand, Ruth said, *"Where you go I will go, where you stay I will stay. Your people will be my people and your God my God. Where you die I will die"* (Ruth 1:16-17). By faith and determination, even though despised as a Moabite, Ruth received the honor of being in the genealogy of Jesus Christ.

Do you have sufficient faith and determination to make the hard decisions?

Adding to Calamity

Because the Lord had closed Hannah's womb [her calamity], her rival kept provoking her in order to irritate her [adding to her calamity]. This went on year after year (1 Sam. 1:6-7).

PERSONAL loss and suffering—calamity—can occur in life. Because God knows everything, He is touched with *the feeling of our infirmity*. Often the devil wants to add to the calamity and the Bible is full of examples including this story of Hannah (see above).

But in all things, God sees the misery of His people; as the Bible says, *"I have indeed seen the misery of my people"* (Exod. 3:7).

Whatever you may be going through, God knows and has all things under control! Be encouraged, God will not stand by and allow evil to add to your sufferings; *"I was only a little angry, but they* [enemies] *added to the calamity"* (Zech. 1:15 NIV 1984). Then He rose to defend Israel.

The word for you today is that God will arise on your behalf and be angry with your enemies!

Does it feel as if your calamity is being intentionally increased?

Famines Don't Last Forever

*In the days when the judges ruled, there was a
famine in the land* (Ruth 1:1).

SEASONS come and go! Even in the Promised Land, a land flowing with milk and honey, God may allow famine to occur.

So there was a famine in the land of Judah (see Ruth 1:1), and a man from Bethlehem, the house of bread, moved to Moab, the land of incest and wickedness! He forgot that hard times don't last forever.

"When Naomi heard in Moab that the LORD had come to the aid of his people by providing food for them, she and her daughters-in-law prepared to return home from there" (Ruth 1:6). In the same, God will provide food for you; He is *"concerned about their sufferings"* (Exod. 3:7).

He will come to your aid if you call on Him. This is divine assurance! May God grant you the wisdom to manage the seasons of your life in accordance with His plans.

**Are you in the middle of a situation that seems
to go on forever?**

The Rock of Escape

Then Saul went on one side of the mountain, and David and his men on the other side of the mountain. So David made haste to get away...[but] Saul and his men were encircling David and his men to take them. But a messenger came to Saul saying...that "Philistines have invaded the land!" Saul returned from pursuing David, and went against the Philistines; so they called that place the Rock of Escape (1 Samuel 23:26-28 NKJV).

G OD does not fight all battles head-on, sometimes He just ignores them until they are burnt out on their own, or He may prefer that two battle situations neutralize each other! Saul wanted to kill David, and the Philistines hated David, so God set them against each other. And in the process, David was able to escape.

May the spirit of infirmity and the spirit of poverty drive each other out of your life and family and create your escape to fullness in God.

How dependent are you on the Rock of Escape?

God Will Turn Your Mistakes Around

On the day the LORD gave the Amorites over to Israel, Joshua said to the LORD in the presence of Israel: "Sun, stand still over Gibeon, and you, moon, over the Valley of Aijalon." So the sun stood still, and the moon stopped, till the nation avenged itself on its enemies (Joshua 10:12-13).

You may know the story about when the sun and the moon stood still for Joshua. But do you know that the event stemmed from a background of grievous mistakes that Joshua had earlier made; but in sincerity and obedience, he gained outstanding victory over his enemies?

This was his mistake, *"when the people of Gibeon heard what Joshua had done to Jericho and Ai, they resorted to a ruse"* (Josh. 9:3-4). They pretended to have come from a distant place and deceived Joshua and formed a treaty with Israel. *"They put worn and patched sandals on their feet and wore old clothes. All the bread of their food supply was dry and moldy. Then they went to Joshua..."We have come from a distant country; make a treaty with us." The Israelites said to the Hivites, "But perhaps you live near us, so how can we make a treaty with you?" The Israelites sampled their provisions but did not inquire of the LORD* (Joshua 9:5-7,14).

Soon after, five kings attacked Gibeon, and Israel was drawn into the war because of the treaty he was deceived into signing. So as not to commit two errors, Joshua decided to stand by that treaty, and it was his commitment to the terms of the treaty that God granted Joshua great success. That was when the sun and moon stood still.

This is what God can do! Be faithful to God, and He will advance you despite your past mistakes!

**What mistakes can you turn over to God
so He can turn them around?**

The Battle Belongs to God

But thanks be to God! **He gives us the victory through our Lord Jesus Christ.** *Therefore, my dear brothers and sisters, stand firm. Let nothing move you. Always give yourselves fully to the work of the Lord, because you know that your labor in the Lord is not in vain* (1 Corinthians 15:56-57).

HEAR this: Jonathan said, *"Nothing can hinder the Lord from saving, whether by many or by few"* (1 Sam. 14:6b); emphasising that your strength may be small at times or *"For it makes no difference to the Lord how many enemy troops there are"* (Living Bible), emphasising that the circumstances may appear overwhelming, but the Lord gives victory!

David said to Goliath, *"All those gathered here will know that it is not by sword or spear that the LORD saves; for the battle is the LORD's"* (1 Sam. 17:47).

May the Lord fight your battles! Amen. Trust in the Lord and He will grant your heart's desires.

Do you believe that the Lord is fighting your battles— and winning?

Let Go of the Past

After the death of Moses the servant of the Lord, the Lord said to Joshua son of Nun, Moses' aide: "Moses my servant is dead. Now then, you and all these people, get ready to cross the Jordan River into the land I am about to give to them—to the Israelites" (Joshua 1:1-2).

MOSES was an outstanding man of God, and Joshua was his faithful aid. But the baton changed hands. Moses is dead, and Joshua has assumed the reign; but Joshua was stuck in the wonderful memories of yesterday until God spoke. If we do not let go of the past, we will never be able to embrace the future—no matter how equipped we may be. The victories of yesterday or even the joyful experiences of the past need to stop occupying the throne of our lives—the central portion of our focus—as if God cannot do greater things.

He can!

If God sits on your throne, He will direct your steps by His Word.

**Is there a memory haunting you,
keeping you from moving ahead?**

Reading the Bible in a Year: 1 Kings 19-20 & John 2.

The Least Are Used by God

So the last [least] *will be first, and the first will be last* (Matthew 20:16).

Gideon said he was the least of his family, *"but how can I save Israel? My clan is the weakest in Manasseh and I am the least in my family"* (Judg. 6:15). Yet God chose him!

David's father thought that he was the least of the sons. But God chose him! Saul felt unqualified to rule Israel, *"But am I not a Benjamite, from the smallest tribe of Israel, and is not my clan the least of all the clans of the tribe of Benjamin? Why do you say such a thing to me?"* (1 Sam. 9:21). Yet he was chosen despite his birth tribe.

Promotion comes from the Lord. God changes the times and the seasons. That is why David said, *"Is not my house chosen by God?"*

Against all odds, God has chosen you and your family to fulfill His purpose! This is the season of divine order in your life.

**Do you feel as if you are the least—
in your family, workplace, church?**

Waiting on God

so she said to Abram, "The LORD has kept me from having children. Go, sleep with my slave; perhaps I can build a family through her." Abram agreed to what Sarai said (Genesis 16:2).

A FTER waiting for a long time for a child, Sarah and Abraham lost patience and got Ishmael—and all the problems associated with that action still persist on earth even to this day! (See Genesis 16:1-11.)

Here is another story; *"Then Samuel took a flask of oil and poured it on Saul's head...saying 'Has not the Lord anointed you leader over His inheritance?'"* (1 Sam. 10:1). Later Samuel told Saul that he must wait for him, *"Go down ahead of me to Gilgal. I will surely come down to you to sacrifice burnt offering, but you must wait seven days until I come to you and tell you what you are to do"* (1 Sam. 10:8). Saul failed because he could not wait (see 1 Sam. 13:7-10). On the other hand, David waited many years and became a man after God's own heart.

Waiting can be the hard part, but may God grant you the grace to wait on Him! Indeed, *"Those who wait on the Lord shall renew their strength"* (Isa. 40:31 NKJV).

Are there things you can do to keep you content while waiting?

Different Types of Altars

*And I heard the altar respond: "Yes, Lord God Almighty, true
and just are your judgments"* (Revelation 16:17).

As mentioned previously, altars are sacred places set aside for communing with the spirit realm, and if used for godly practices according to godly principles, they are good places.

In Bible days, some altars were built as places where people could go to remind themselves of what God did in the past and to honor Him. They also provide a rally point in times of challenges and a reference point for posterity. One lasting testimony we can leave is to build altars as thanksgiving for His mercy and goodness in our lives, for instance:

- *"Moses built an altar and called it **The Lord is my Banner**"* (Exod. 17:15). May His banner of love continue to be over you.

- *"So Gideon built an altar to the Lord there and called it **The Lord is Peace**"* (Judg. 6:24). May His peace be your guide always.

- *"Then Samuel took a stone and set it up between Mizpah and Shen. He named it Ebenezer, saying '**Thus far has the Lord helped us**'"* (1 Sam. 7:12). May God continue to be your ever-present help in times of need.

- *"Today I* [the Lord] *have rolled away the reproach of the past from you. So the place has been called Gilgal to this day"* (Josh. 5:9). May you continue to be the fragrance of the aroma of Christ. No more shame, no more disgrace, no more failure but honor and glory shall clothe you.

**Is there a place in your home where you could build
an altar to His goodness and mercy?**

Help Comes from Unexpected Sources

*The king of Israel replied, "If the LORD does **not help you,** where can I get help for you? From the threshing floor? From the winepress?"* (2 Kings 6:27)

MANY people are fixed on where they expect help to come from. But if God does not send help, where can anyone get help? God can send help through unexpected means. Here are the stories of two servants who made the difference in the lives of two great people.

Saul's servant said, *"Look, in this town there is a man of God; he is highly respected, and everything he says comes true. Let go there now. Perhaps he will tell us what way to take"* (1 Sam. 9:6). The rest of the story is history. Saul did, and in the process Saul became the first king of Israel.

Naaman's servant said, *"If only my master would see the prophet who is in Samaria! He would cure him of his leprosy"* (2 Kings 5:3). Naaman did, and yes indeed he was cured.

May God's voice and help come to you no matter how!

Are you expecting help from expected sources?

Keeping God's Commandments

*You shall not bow down to them or worship them; for I, the LORD your God, am a jealous God, punishing the children for the sin of the parents to the third and fourth generation of those who hate me, but showing love to a thousand generations of **those who love me and keep my commandments*** (Deuteronomy 5:9-11).

THE Book of Ecclesiastes states that to fear God and keep His commandment is the essence of humankind! That is why the prophet Hanani said, *"For the eyes of the Lord range throughout the earth to strengthen those whose hearts are **fully committed to him***" (2 Chron. 16:9).

And Samuel said to Saul, *"the Lord has sought out a man after His own heart and appointed him ruler of His people, because **you have not kept the Lord's command***" (1 Sam. 13:14b).

Later, Samuel admonished that *"To obey is better than sacrifice...for rebellion is like the sin of divination* [witchcraft]" (1 Sam. 15:22-23).

Obey God no matter the pressure of the day. It is also true that the measure to which you keep His command is the measure to which your heart is committed to Him!

Are some commandments easier to keep than others?

The Cave of Adullam

David left Gath and escaped to the cave of Adullam. When his brothers and his father's household heard about it, they went to him there. All those who were in distress or in debt or discontented gathered around him, and he became their commander (1 Samuel 22:1-2).

THE cave of Adullam was an ordinary cave, but it was also a place of transformation where mighty men were made out of the rejects of the society. How did this happen in an ordinary cave? There are many reasons including the anointing, loyalty, leadership, commitment to a common purpose, and trust in God from whom all these blessings flow!

These rejects became the mighty men of David—men who did extraordinary exploits for God! God can use anyone for great things irrespective of the person's background or weaknesses.

Trust in God, He transforms people.

Are you in need of transformation?

Financial Anointing

Isaac planted crops in that land [during the famine] *and the same year reaped a hundredfold, because the LORD blessed him. The man became rich, and his wealth continued to grow until he became very wealthy* (Genesis 26:12-13).

Today is a day for an apostolic transfer of divine ability for financial anointing. Just as Moses instructed the Israelites, *"The Israelites did as Moses instructed and asked the Egyptians for articles of silver and gold and for clothing. The LORD had made the Egyptians favorably disposed toward the people, and they gave them what they asked for"* (Exod. 12:35-36).

Elijah, also under the apostolic unction decreed, *"the jar of flour will not be used up and the jug of oil will not run dry"* (1 Kings 17:14). And it came to pass! So it shall be for you—abundance instead of starvation.

Under the same unction, the prophet Elisha proclaimed, *"Go, sell the oil and pay your debts. You and your sons can live on what is left"* (2 Kings 4:7). So also there will be divine cancellation of debts for you.

I pray that you become wealthy and will not be hindered by the global economic recession.

Has your nation's financial crisis impacted you?

Don't Let Greed Spoil Your Victory

*But all the evil men and troublemakers among David's fol-
lowers said, "Because they did not go out with us, we will not
share with them the plunder we recovered." ...David replied
"No my brothers, you must not do that with what the LORD
has given us. ...All will share alike"* (1 Samuel 30:22-24).

MANY people have been stripped off their full harvest because
they could not manage the initial phase of their reward.
Remember, if God can trust you with a little, He will give you charge
over much! The Bible described certain people as evil and troublemakers because of their greed! (See Scripture above.)

Later, David *"sent some of the plunder to the elders of Judah"* (1 Sam.
30:26). Many people never really attain the fullness of their blessing
because they disregard spiritual principles. Whatever potential or
giftedness that the Lord has given you, it is first and foremost for the
Body of Christ.

You will attain your fullness when greed is not part of your
mindset.

Everyone has a greedy streak.
Can you keep yours under control?

Raising Your Voice with Others

*How good and pleasant it is when God's people **live together in unity!** It is like precious oil poured on the head, running down on the beard.... It is as if the dew of Hermon were falling on Mount Zion. For there the LORD bestows his blessing, even life forevermore* (Psalm 133:1-3).

THERE is power in unity no matter at what level it is exercised. The power inherent in unity was displayed in the church of the Acts of the apostles:

*On their release, Peter and John went back to their own people and reported all that the chief priests and the elders had said to them. When they heard this, **they raised their voices together in prayer to God.** "Sovereign Lord," they said, "you made the heavens and the earth and the sea, and everything in them. ...Now, Lord, consider their threats and enable your servants to speak your word with great boldness. Stretch out your hand to heal and perform signs and wonders through the name of your holy servant Jesus." After they prayed, the place where they were meeting was shaken. And **they were all filled with the Holy Spirit and spoke the word of God boldly. All the believers were one in heart and mind.** ...And **God's grace was so powerfully at work in them all**"* (Acts 4:23-33).

The main points: 1) "Lord consider their threats"; 2) "enable Your servants to speak Your word with boldness"; 3) "Stretch out Your hand to heal"; 4) "perform miraculous signs and wonders through the name of Holy Son Jesus"; 5) Pour out Your Holy Spirit and fill us with Your glory.

As you make all efforts to bring unity, may these blessings be upon you.

How important is unity to you?

Reading the Bible in a Year: 2 Kings 20-22 & John 6:45-71.

Blessings in His Presence

You will show me the path of life; in Your presence is fullness of joy; at Your right hand are pleasures forevermore
(Psalm 16:11 NKJV).

THERE are blessings in His presence.

The household of Obed-Edom surely knew and saw this principle in action: "*The ark of the Lord remained in the house of Obed-Edom... and the Lord blessed him and his entire household. Now King David was told...So David went to bring up the ark of God from the house of Obed -Edom to the City of David with rejoicing*" (2 Sam. 6:11-12).

As a result of Obed-Edom's blessings, the consciousness of the nation was awakened to the awesome presence of God and His blessings.

May your blessings make you rich and add no sorrow. May your blessings make the difference in your generation!

**Have you experienced fullness of joy
in His presence?**

Take Spiritual Threats Seriously

So we fix our eyes not on what is seen, but on what is unseen, since what is seen is temporary, but what is unseen is eternal (2 Corinthians 4:18).

THE Bible says what is seen was made from what was invisible. King David experienced this principle in action, and he responded to it appropriately. David and his men marched to capture Jerusalem after he was made king of Israel. But the inhabitants, the Jebusites, issued a spiritual threat in the form of verbal curse, *"You will not get in here; even the blind and the lame can ward you off." ... Nevertheless David captured the fortress of Zion, which is the City of David"* (2 Sam. 5:6-7).

Then David did something remarkable, he issued a counter spiritual pronouncement, *"That is why they say, 'The blind and lame' will not enter the palace"* (2 Sam. 5:8).

Send your word back to counter and neutralize the potential dangers of the enemy's curse! Use passages like Amos 7:1-2 for every threat against you, seen or unseen. To Amos, the Lord said about such potential danger, *"This will not happen"*—and this what He is saying today to you.

Are your eyes fixed on the seen or the unseen?

Be Fervent in Serving the Lord

When those who were carrying the ark of the LORD had taken six steps, he sacrificed a bull and a fattened calf. Wearing a linen ephod, David was dancing before the LORD with all his might, while he and all Israel were bringing up the ark of the LORD with shouts and the sound of trumpets (2 Samuel 6:13-15).

WHEN David heard that the Lord had blessed the house of Obed-Edom, he brought the ark of God to the City of David with great celebration, enthusiasm, and spiritual fervency! The Bible says this is fervency put into action.

God established David's throne as an everlasting throne because of his reverence for the ark—God's presence. God will bless your spiritual fervency, too. Let the zeal of the Lord be your portion, and His zeal will accomplish His plans for your life. Be fervent serving the Lord; there is great reward!

How fervent are you?

God Speaks through Your Mind

The Spirit of the Lord will come powerfully upon you, and you will prophesy with them. You will be changed into a different person. Once these signs are fulfilled, do whatever your hand finds to do, for God is with you (1 Samuel 10:6-7).

GOD may speak to you in whatever way He chooses. Often He speaks into people's minds particularly when they have the mind of Christ. Here are some instances when people moved according to their mind as they were inspired by God, "Nathan replied to the king [David], "Whatever you have in mind, go ahead and do it, for the Lord is with you" (2 Sam. 7:3).

The key in these passages is that your mind is usable by God only if:

- The Lord is with you.
- You have peace with God.
- You regard no iniquity in your heart.
- You have the love of God in your heart.
- It lines up with Scripture.

Is God speaking to you?

Fighting with Yesterday's Mandate

Once more the Philistines came up and spread out in the Valley of Rephaim, so David inquired of the Lord and He answered... (2 Samuel 5:22-23).

G OD gave David order and strategy to defeat the Philistines. But soon after that victory, the Philistines came up again. Rather than assume power from yesterday's mandate, David sought a fresh one, even though the second battle was immediately after the victory of the first battle.

This was wise of David, as God had a new and different strategy for David. The result, *"David did as the LORD commanded him, and he struck down the Philistines all the way from Gibeon to Gezer"* (2 Sam. 5:25).

Fresh mandate, new strategy, and greater victory!

Pray daily for a fresh mandate from the King of kings.

Will you ask for and then listen for God's mandate?

Inheriting Past Treasures

When Mephibosheth son of Jonathan, the son of Saul, came to David, he bowed down to pay him honor. David said..."Don't be afraid," David said to him, "for I will surely show you kindness for the sake of your father Jonathan. I will restore to you all the land that belonged to your grandfather Saul, and you will always eat at my table" (2 Samuel 9:6-7).

M EPHIBOSHETH was not only restored, he was also promoted to royalty and gained the status of sonship with King David. In just one day he rose from a place of rejection to the palace in Jerusalem, the city of God.

May the goodness of your parents speak for you and live after you.

**Do you expect your parents' legacy
to speak highly for you?**

Prayer Against Evil

When King Jeroboam heard what the man of God cried out against the altar at Bethel, he stretched out his hand from the altar and said, "Seize him!" But the hand he stretched out toward the man shriveled up, so that he could not pull it back. Also, the altar was split apart and its ashes poured out according to the sign given by the man of God by the word of the LORD. Then the king said to the man of God, "Intercede with the LORD your God and pray for me that my hand may be restored." So the man of God interceded with the LORD, and the king's hand was restored and became as it was before (1 Kings 13:4-6).

E VERY pronouncement and intention of the evil priest of the ancient ungodly altar shall be frustrated and disappointed by God, *"By the word of the LORD a man of God came from Judah to Bethel, as Jeroboam was standing by the altar to make an offering"* (1 Kings 13:1).

May the word of God come against the satanic altar and the evil priests; may their bones be sacrificed on their altar, *"He cried out against the altar by the word of the LORD: **"Altar, altar!** This is what the LORD says: 'A son named Josiah will be born to the house of David. On you he will sacrifice the priests of the high places who now make offerings here, and human bones will be burned on you'"* (1 Kings 13:2).

I pray that any evil force or evil ruler of darkness that may take your matter to the altar will have his or her hand shriveled up and not returned its normal position. May the power of God prevail against the power at the evil altar, and that the priests and the evil worshipers will submit to God—and He subdues them in your behalf.

Are you afraid of evil?

Prayers for the Restoration of God's Altar

Then Elijah said to all the people, "Come here to me." They came to him, and he repaired the altar of the LORD, which had been torn down. Elijah took twelve stones, one for each of the tribes descended from Jacob, to whom the word of the LORD had come, saying, "Your name shall be Israel." With the stones he built an altar in the name of the LORD, and he dug a trench around it...The water ran down around the altar and even filled the trench. At the time of sacrifice, the prophet Elijah stepped forward and prayed: "LORD, the God of Abraham, Isaac and Israel, let it be known today that you are God in Israel and that I am your servant and have done all these things at your command. Answer me, LORD, answer me, so these people will know that you, LORD, are God, and that you are turning their hearts back again." Then the fire of the LORD fell and burned up the sacrifice, the wood, the stones and the soil, and also licked up the water in the trench. When all the people saw this, they fell prostrate and cried, "The LORD—he is God! The LORD—he is God!" (1 Kings 18:30-39)

MAY the people come together and be obedient to the priest of God. May the ancient ruins of the altar of God be repaired.

May the foundation of God's altar be repaired, and may the original purpose and destiny of His people be restored. May the right prayers be offered at the altar and the God who answers by fire, let Him be God.

Your Lord is God—may you always be mindful of His sovereignty.

What does restoring His altar mean to you?

Prayers Against Witchcraft

Let no one be found among you who sacrifices their son or daughter in the fire, who practices divination or sorcery, interprets omens, engages in witchcraft, or casts spells, or who is a medium or spiritist or who consults the dead. Anyone who does these things is detestable to the LORD; because of these same detestable practices the LORD your God will drive out those nations before you (Deuteronomy 18:10-12).

G OD will root out every act of witchcraft. May the Lord's anger be provoked against any practice and act of witchcraft against you, your family, and your ministry-career, *"He sacrificed his children in the fire in the Valley of Ben Hinnom, practiced divination and witchcraft, sought omens, and consulted mediums and spiritists. He did much evil in the eyes of the LORD, arousing his anger"* (2 Chron. 33:6).

May God's peace prevail over the fear generated by acts of witchcraft. May God's peace drive out the cloud of confusion associated with spells of the acts of witchcraft; *"When Joram saw Jehu he asked, "Have you come in peace, Jehu?" "How can there be peace," Jehu replied, "as long as all the idolatry and witchcraft of your mother Jezebel abound"* (2 Kings 9:22).

Every act of witchcraft is banished from your bloodline (see Exod. 22:18). God! Destroy the generational stain and acts of witchcraft that may come against believers, *"In that day," declares the LORD, "I will destroy...your witchcraft and you will no longer cast spells. I will destroy your idols and your sacred stones from among you; you will no longer bow down to the work of your hands. I will uproot from among you your Asherah poles when I demolish your cities"* (Micah 5:10-14).

Can you stand strong against this enemy?

Additional Prayers against Witchcraft

I pray that any bondage initiated and maintained by the acts of witchcraft is hereby broken, *"All because of the wanton lust of a prostitute, alluring, the mistress of sorceries, who **enslaved** nations by her prostitution and peoples by her witchcraft. 'I am against you' declares the Lord Almighty..."* (Nahum 3:4-5).

I pray that you will resist the spirit of rebellion against God, *"For **rebellion is like the sin of divination** [witchcraft], and arrogance like the evil of idolatry. Because you have rejected the word of the LORD, he has rejected you as king"* (1 Samuel 15:23).

I pray that you are filled and led by the Spirit of God; there is no room for the acts of witchcraft in your life and family; I replace any mark or remnants of the practice of witchcraft in the past generation of your bloodline with the fruit of the Spirit, *"But **if you are led by the Spirit,** you are not under law. **The acts of the sinful nature are obvious**: sexual immorality, impurity and debauchery; idolatry and witchcraft; hatred, discord, jealousy, fits of rage, selfish ambition, dissensions, factions and envy; drunkenness, orgies, and the like. I warn you, as I did before, that those who live like this will not inherit the kingdom of God. But **the fruit of the Spirit is love, joy peace, patience, kindness, goodness, faithfulness**"* (Gal. 5:18-22).

Are you as fruitful as you can be?

Every Good Promise Is Surrounded by Giants

David was greatly distressed because the men were talking of stoning him; each one was bitter in spirit because of his sons and daughters. But David found strength in the LORD his God. Then...David inquired of the LORD, "Shall I pursue this raiding party? Will I overtake them?" "Pursue them," he answered. "You will certainly overtake them and succeed in the rescue" (1 Samuel 30:6-8).

DAVID and his men wept bitterly about the loss of their families and homes; and David was in great distress because the men were talking of stoning him! On inquiry, the Lord said, *"Pursue them...You will certainly overtake them and succeed in the rescue"* (1 Sam. 30:8).

But God did tell him that it was going to be a long and hard-to-fight battle; *"David fought them from dusk until the evening of the next day!* (1 Sam. 30:17).

David succeeded as he was promised; but in reality, he fought his way into this promise. Work the divine promises over you into the realities of your life.

Are you willing to fight to secure your good promise from God?

Uncommon Wisdom

When all Israel heard the verdict the king had given, they held the king in awe, because they saw that he had wisdom from God (1 Kings 3:28).

T HE wisdom that the king displayed is uncommon wisdom in action. God gives you this wisdom as well.

For I will give you words and wisdom that none of your adversaries [contemporaries] *will be able to resist or contradict* (Luke 21:15).

Uncommon wisdom is able to break all barriers, defeat all contradictions, and advance your plans. May God grant you uncommon wisdom that everyone will realize that the hand of God is in it.

May the Lord grant you this wisdom to apply to your family and other relationships, marriage, career, and all of life's decisions.

Have you experienced uncommon wisdom?

With the Ark Comes Blessings

*But **seek first his kingdom and his righteousness**, and all these things will be given to you as well* (Matthew 6:33).

THIS is the story of when King David first set the Ark in its place and then the people were blessed:

They brought the ark of the Lord and set it in its place inside the tent...After he had finished sacrificing the burnt offerings and fellowship offerings, he blessed the people in the name of the Lord Almighty. Then he gave

~ *a loaf of bread* [meaning divine provision],

~ *a cake of dates* [meaning no one will miss his or set time] *and*

~ *a cake of raisins* [meaning fruitfulness]

to each person in the whole crowd of Israelites, both men and women. And all the people went to their homes. ...David returned home to bless his household... (2 Samuel 6:17-20).

Put God first and everything will fall in place.

Is seeking God's Kingdom and righteousness first in your life?

God Is Worth the Sacrifice

*For God so loved the world that **he gave** his one and only*
Son, that whoever believes in him shall not perish
but have eternal life (John 3:16).

THIS is how the Bible puts it: *"Gather My saints together to Me, those who have made a covenant with Me by sacrifice"* (Ps. 50:5 NKJV). That means giving up something or comfort for something considered valuable.

David said, *"No, I insist on paying you for it. I will not sacrifice to the Lord my God burnt offerings that cost me nothing"* (2 Sam. 24:24). When you are willing to make a sacrifice for God, it shows the value of your relationship with God.

**Consider what you can give to advance
the Kingdom of God.**

No Limitations with God

The king [David] asked, "Is there no one still alive from the house of Saul to whom I can show God's kindness?" Ziba answered the king, "There is still a son of Jonathan; he is lame in both feet." "Where is he?" the king asked. Ziba answered, "He is at the house of Makir son of Ammiel in Lo Debar (2 Samuel 9:3-4).

S OME are born with limitations, others have limitations thrown at them, but God is able to deliver from them all! No matter if those limitations are physical, emotional, financial, educational, or whatever you think may be holding you back.

The story in Second Samuel is of Jonathan's son. Jonathan's son was not born crippled nor did he become crippled because of his own fault. As a baby, he was accidently dropped by a well-wisher and became crippled. He ended up in a city with poor repudiation and regarded himself as a "dog." But God broke through for him and promoted him to royalty despite his crippled feet. *"Melphibosheth lived in Jerusalem, because he always ate at the king's table and he was lame [crippled] in both feet"* (2 Sam. 9:13).

Promotion in life comes from God. There is nothing that can hinder God from moving you ahead in life if that is His will.

Do you feel crippled in some way?

The True Spirit of Commitment

The king [David] asked, "Is there no one still alive from the house of Saul to whom I can show God's kindness?"
(2 Samuel 9:3).

DAVID asked if there was anyone still left of the house of Saul to whom he could show kindness to—for his dear friend's Jonathan sake. David had a covenant with Jonathan and this was outstanding in many respects.

There was a genuine love between David and Jonathan, without sexual overtone. Though Jonathan was now dead, and David had become the most powerful man in the kingdom as the king, he remembered his covenant with Jonathan. He was committed to the covenant no matter what.

This was a true show of character, integrity, and spirituality of David—who came to be known as a man after God's heart.

Stand strong by your word.

Is there someone you need to follow-up with regarding a covenant?

Your Real Name

Now there was a servant of Saul's household named Ziba. They summoned him to appear before David and the king said to him, "Are you Ziba?" (2 Samuel 9:2).

THE king did not ask him, "Are you the servant of Saul?" No. He called him by his real name!

From that moment, he was no longer a servant to another man but a manager of great resources, the estate of King Saul. Ziba stood before the king a new person with his real name. This is what one day of living in God's presence can bring in the life of a person.

*She will give birth to a son, and you are to give him the **name Jesus**, because he will save his people from their sins* (Matthew 1:21).

How does it make you feel when someone respectfully calls you by your name?

Reading the Bible in a Year: 2 Chronicles 13-16 & John 14.

People United Under God

The people of Judah and Israel were as numerous as the sand on the seashore; **they ate, they drank and they were happy***. And Solomon ruled over all the kingdoms from the River to the land of Philistines, as far as the border of Egypt...*
(1 Kings 4:20-21).

THIS is the picture of a united Israel and Judah in the early days of the kingship of Solomon.

The picture of a people:

- numerous as the sand on the seashore
- eating
- drinking
- being happy
- under one kingship
- enjoying peace on all sides
- living in safety
- under their own vines and fig trees
- who were lacking nothing in their midst

This is my prayer for you, your family, and your country!

How united do you feel with others in your church, community, region, nation?

The Wisdom of Solomon

*God gave **Solomon wisdom** and very great insight, and a breadth of understanding as measureless as the sand on the seashore* (1 Kings 4:29).

God gave Solomon wisdom that was remarkable. Solomon was outstanding in many ways, particularly in the way he asked for wisdom instead of riches or the life of his enemies. He was focused; the wisdom he wanted was to help him carry out God's agenda on earth. God was pleased by this, and He added many other things to his request.

Here are some of the characteristics of this great wisdom:

- Great insight into people and situations
- Breadth of understanding
- Greater than the wisdom of all the wise men of the East
- Spoke 3,000 proverbs
- His songs numbered 1,005
- Described plant life
- Taught about animals, birds, reptiles, and fish
- People of all nations came to listen to his wisdom

May God grant you this rare form of wisdom!

What is the first thing you would do if you had Solomon's wisdom?

Wars from all Sides

You know that because of the wars waged against my father
David from all sides...until the Lord put his enemies
under his feet (1 Kings 5:3).

EVEN David, despite his special relationship with God, had to fight wars "from all sides"; but in all, God defeated his enemies in whatever shape or form they came at him.

Whatever challenge you may be facing right now, be assured it is not a sign that you are in the wrong place or that God did not send you. For David, that was how he became a man after God's heart.

A challenge is the precursor for victory. God will fight your battles!

**Does it sometimes feel as if there are wars
raging on all sides of you?**

Rest on Every Side

Now the Lord my God has given me rest on every side, and there is no adversary or disaster. I intend therefore, to build a temple for the name of the Lord my God (1 Kings 5:4).

SOLOMON said that his God gave him rest on every side—he had peace and security. What did he say after that? He was going to build a temple for God in appreciation for His faithfulness.

The Lord gives power to succeed. When God gave Solomon peace and rest, in the midst of the luxury, he remembered God—he appreciated what He had done for him.

Remember to thank God when it is well with you, and it will continue to be well with you.

What is it today that you need to thank God for?

Distinguished by Your Skills

You know that we have no one so skilled in felling timber as the Sidonians (1 Kings 5:6b).

GOD gives the potentials for skills, but we are responsible for developing the skills. The Sidonians were well-known for their skills in forestry. Solomon paid tribute to their unusual ability.

Your *gifts* will make way for you too, but your *skills* will keep you a step above your peers! Work on your abilities and develop your skills, and your skills will distinguish you from others.

**What steps do you need to take to
fully develop your skills?**

Don't Stop at Your First Victory Post

Roll large rocks up to the mouth of the cave, and post some men there to guard it. **But don't stop!** *Pursue your enemies, attack them from the rear and don't let them reach their cities for God has given them into your hands* (Joshua 10:17-19).

WHEN Joshua was told that his enemies—the five kings combined to wage war against him—were found hiding in a cave, Joshua said to his men to close the opening of the cave but not to stop there.

In those days, when the king was captured, the war was over. But Joshua was determined to root out even future threats after trapping the five kings!

Do not stop at the first sign of victory—always bring your victory to the logical conclusion.

**Do you need to take some logical steps
to finalize your victory?**

Riding on Divine Momentum

...Joshua said to the LORD in the presence of Israel: "Sun, stand still over Gibeon, and you, moon, over the Valley of Aijalon." So the sun stood still, and the moon stopped, till the nation avenged itself on its enemies (Joshua 10:12-13).

JOSHUA made this classic request of the Lord on the day God gave him great victory over the Amorites.

The sun delayed going down about a full day so Joshua could maximize his victory. The Bible says there has never been a day like that before—surely the Lord was fighting for Israel.

May the Lord grant you victory and allow you to ride on the crest of His momentum.

Are you buckled up and ready to take a ride on His divine momentum?

Complete what You Start

*And they exceeded our expectations: They gave themselves first of all to the Lord, and then by the will of God also to us. So we urged Titus, just as he had earlier made a beginning, to **bring also to completion** this act of grace on your part* (2 Corinthians 8:5-6).

THE Bible emphasizes the fact that Solomon began and completed the magnificent temple he built for God:

- *the temple was finished in all its details according to its specifications. He had spent seven years building it* (1 Kings 6:38).

- *So he built the temple and completed it, roofing it with beams and cedar planks* (1 Kings 6:9).

- *So Solomon built the temple and completed it* (1 Kings 6:14).

May you complete the work of your hands. It is best to seek God about all the projects you started and never finished. Maybe there are some that need to be forgotten, and others that need to be completed. Use your time wisely.

As God promised Zerubbabel, *"The hands of Zerubbabel have laid the foundation of this temple; his hands will also complete it"* (Zech. 4:9), so the Lord promises toward you!

Is there any unfinished work or business you need to complete?

The Power of Your Thought Life

*But the LORD said to my father David, "You did well to
have it in your heart to build a temple for my Name"*
(1 Kings 8:18).

GOD places high premium on the thoughts of our hearts; our
actions are predicated on our thoughts.

Even our whole world is woven around the issues that occupy
our hearts, *"Keep your heart with all diligence, for out of it spring the
issues of life"* (Prov. 4:23 NKJV).

This is a fact of life, *"For as he thinks in his heart, so is he"* (Prov.
23:7 NKJV). What have you been thinking lately?

I pray that *"the peace of God, which transcends all understanding,
will guard your hearts and minds in Christ Jesus"* (Phil. 4:7).

Is your mind at peace?

Cry and Prayer

Yet give attention to your servant's prayer and his plea for mercy, LORD my God. Hear the cry and the prayer that your servant is praying in your presence this day (1 Kings 8:28).

Your cry will pray for you! Indeed, Solomon described the cry of his heart as praying.

And the psalmist said, *"Hear my cry, O God. Attend to my prayer. From the end of the earth I will cry to You, when my heart is overwhelmed; lead me to the rock that is higher than I"* (Ps. 61:1-2 NKJV). This person cried unto God, the Lord heard him and delivered him from all his troubles.

Not a single drop of tears you have shed is wasted; your tears continue to pray for you, because they are stored in His bottle in Heaven, *"You number my wanderings; put my tears into Your bottle; are they not in Your book?"* (Ps. 56:8 NKJV).

Remember also, *"They who sow in tears, shall reap in joy"* (Ps. 126:5 NKJV). May the Lord hear your cry and reward your tears.

Did you know that God puts your tears into His bottle in Heaven?

Judgment Begins in God's House

Judge between your servants, condemning the guilty and bringing down on his own head what he has done. Declare the innocent not guilty, and so establish his innocence
(1 Kings 8:32b).

Wise King Solomon wrote this Scripture passage in First Kings. The godly shall not be condemned with the ungodly. The Lord will differentiate those who serve Him and those who serve Him not.

In many churches there are those who judge others by using subjective criteria. We must be careful not to usurp God's role as the ultimate Judge and jury. He is the only One who knows the entire story, the intimate details, and the hidden secrets within a person's heart and mind.

Have you been wrongly judged?

The God of Miracles

Great crowds came to him [Jesus], *bringing the lame, the blind, the crippled, the mute and many others, and laid them at his feet; and he healed them. The people were amazed when they saw the mute speaking, the crippled made well, the lame walking and the blind seeing. And they praised the God of Israel* (Matthew 15:30-31).

THIS is the true manifestation of the Kingdom of God on earth. As the Bible says, *"the kingdom of God is not a matter of talk but of power."* May the Lord turn your impossibility into possibility! With Him nothing is impossible.

May this awesome power of God be manifested in your life, family, church, career, and community.

Have you been amazed at God's miracles recently?

The Sound of Abundant Rain

"Go up, eat and drink, for there is the sound of abundance of rain" (1 Kings 18:41 NKJV).

THESE are the words of Prophet Elijah to King Ahab and the people of Israel that signal the end of a difficult period in their history. He was telling them that the famine, the draught, is coming to an end and the rain—the abundance of blessings will come upon the people!

A word from God can change your life. In this case, God spoke through Elijah. No hard times last forever; God will give you abundance instead of draught.

Let these words light up in your spirit today.

Are you listening for the sound of abundant rain?

There Is a River

*On the last and greatest day of the festival, Jesus stood and said in a loud voice, "Let anyone who is thirsty come to me and drink. Whoever believes in me, as Scripture has said, **rivers of living water will flow from within them**"*
(John 7:37-38).

A s a person redeemed of the Lord, there is a river inside you.
The Bible describes the river of living water as springing up from the believer. Let this water spring from within you to wash over every situation or person who may came across your path and bring life to them.

And the psalmist also says that, *"There is a river whose streams make glad the city of God, the holy place where the Most High dwells. God is within her, she will not fall; God will help her at break of day"* (Ps. 46:4-5).

The river in you is your source of eternal joy! Out of it flows the help you need!

Is your river flowing in the right direction?

Purpose, Dominance, Prominence

Jesus looked at them and said, "With man this is impossible,
but with God all things are possible" (Matthew 19:26).

THESE words of Jesus to His disciples echo in my spirit morning by morning. They will never fail you, as well. We do not achieve our goals with human means! God is able to do it for you.

God gives success no matter your actual physical or mental strength, big or small. The Bible says, *"As long as he* [Uzziah] *sought the Lord, God gave him success"* (2 Chron. 26:5b).

Commitment to God gives you the drive to your divine purpose in life, your purpose leads you to the place of dominance, and dominance gives prominence. Such is a key to life of purpose to those who find it. That is why *"the eyes of the Lord range throughout the earth to strengthen those whose hearts are fully committed to him"* (2 Chron. 16:9).

Are you using this key to open doors
leading to your God-given destiny?

Pray for His Presence and Glory

For the earth will be filled with the knowledge of the glory of the Lord as the waters cover the sea (Habakkuk 2:14).

L ET us pray for the presence of God and for His glory to be poured out on you. This is a divine promise!

We are reminded in the following Bible examples:

- The pillar of fire and pillar of cloud led Jews out of Egypt. Pray that He will lead you by His presence.

- Moses said, *"what else will distinguish me and your people" from others on the surface of the earth"* (Exod. 33:16). His presence, of course!

- The "tongues of fire" on the day of Pentecost (see Acts 2); the birth of the church of Christ. His presence will birth new depths of God into our lives.

I pray that you will feel His presence daily as you go about your routines. I also pray that His glory will surround you throughout the day and night—while awake and while asleep.

Is there a yearning in your spirit for His presence and His glory?

Divine Arrangements

Go into the village over there," he said. "As soon as you enter it, you will see a donkey tied there, with its colt beside it. Untie them and bring them to me. If anyone asks what you are doing, just say, 'The Lord needs them,' and he will immediately let you take them." This took place to fulfill the prophecy...
(Matthew 21:2-4).

G OD is able to rearrange events and circumstances concerning you to bring fulfillment to His prophecy in your life.

May you take steps today to move into your destiny. May you recognize His divine arrangements when you see them. Pray for a spirit of discernment so you can walk in His righteous path.

Are you actively searching for His divine plan for your life?

Help Comes from God

*They were all filled with awe and praised **God**. "A great prophet has appeared among us," they said. "**God** has come to **help** his people"* (Luke 7:16).

*The widow who is really in need and left all alone puts her hope in **God** and continues night and day to pray and to ask **God** for **help*** (1 Timothy 5:5).

*Let us then approach **God**'s throne of grace with confidence, so that we may receive mercy and find grace to **help** us in our time of need* (Hebrews 4:16).

HELP comes from God; and if the Lord does not send help, all efforts are futile.

If God be for you, no one can be against you.

Seeking help from God is the fastest way to overcome any situation.

Life's Difficult Options

*Now there were four men with leprosy at the entrance of the city gate. They said to each other, "**Why stay here until we die?** If we say, 'We'll go into the city'—the famine is there, and we will die. And if we stay here, we will die. So let's go over to the camp of the Arameans and surrender. If they spare us, we live; if they kill us, then we die"* (2 Kings 7:3-4).

THIS is the wisdom of the four lepers—the ones everyone gave up on. Their challenge was daunting to say the least. In the best of times, they begged for alms, but when there was severe famine, they were destined to die before anyone else.

This is their logic—they had three options, which, unfortunately, led to a high probability of cruel death. However, one had a very slight chance of possible survival but could also lead to the quickest death. That option offered immediate death or life. They opted to take that chance by faith and went into the camp of the enemy.

God granted them a miraculous survival based on their faith. They survived and also saved the nation on that day. Often life presents no easy options, but God always answers faith in Him.

**How good are you at weighing all
the options before you make a decision?**

Miracle at Dusk

At dusk they got up and went to the camp of the Arameans. When they reached the edge of the camp, no one was there, for the Lord had caused the Arameans to hear the sound of chariots and horses and a great army, so that they said to one another, "Look, the king of Israel has hired the Hittite and Egyptian kings to attack us!" **So they got up and fled in the dusk** and abandoned their tents and their horses and donkeys. They left the camp as it was and ran for their lives (2 Kings 7:5-7).

THIS is the miracle at dusk! God changed the footsteps of leprous legs to the sound of an approaching mighty great army! At dusk, three things happened, 1) the lepers got up by faith, 2) the Arameans heard the sound of an approaching great army, 3) and they fled leaving their resources for the lepers.

Indeed, the righteous shall live by faith!

Are you living by faith?

Nothing Happens by Chance

At the end of the seven years she came back from the land of the Philistines and went to appeal to the king for her house and land. The king was talking to Gehazi, the servant of the man of God, and had said, "Tell me about all the great things Elisha has done." Just as Gehazi was telling the king how Elisha had restored the dead to life, the woman whose son Elisha had brought back to life came to appeal to the king for her house and land. Gehazi said, "This is the woman, my lord the king, and this is her son whom Elisha restored to life." The king asked the woman about it, and she told him. Then he assigned an official to her case and said to him, "Give back everything that belonged to her, including all the income from her land from the day she left the country until now" (2 Kings 8:3-6).

MANY times God rearranges events in our lives to fulfill His purpose. He may choose to do this by sending His angels or He may use other means. On our part, we should be alert to avail ourselves of such opportunities. This story from Second Kings is of a faithful woman whom I believe God arranged things to bring her to a future and a hope.

God instigated her sojourn in the land of the Philistines and when the famine was over, it was God who arranged events to facilitate the restoration of her land and properties. God is the Author and Finisher of our faith. When He begins a work, He brings it to a perfect conclusion. The Lord will help you today and every day!

Do you agree that nothing happens by chance?

Honor Comes from the Lord

*David said to Michal, "It was before the LORD, who...
appointed me ruler over the LORD's people Israel—I will
celebrate before the LORD. I will become even more undig-
nified than this, and I will be humiliated in my own eyes.
But by these slave girls you spoke of, I will be held in honor"*
(2 Samuel 6:21-22).

HONOR comes from the Lord; He lifts one up and takes another down! David knew this.

God gave Joshua honor before the Israelites, *"And the LORD said to Joshua, "Today I will begin to exalt you in the eyes of all Israel, so they may know that I am with you as I was with Moses"* (Josh. 3:7).

May the Lord honor you and blot out every reproach in your life.

What does honor mean to you?
Who do you honor?

The Days of Your Sorrow will End

Your sun will never set again, and your moon will wane no more, the Lord will be your everlasting light, and the days of your sorrow will end (Isaiah 60:20).

THERE are many benefits of the glory of God's presence. One such benefit is that metaphorically your sun will never set again. This means the end of "boom and burst" circles in your victorious living.

And know indeed that, *"Nations will come to your light and kings to the brightness of your dawn* [up rising]" (Isa. 60:3).

May you have victories on every side. May the Lord be your everlasting Light—shining the way into a life of abundance and grace. May the days of your sorrow end—today. And may you rise and walk in confidence that your heavenly Father loves you deeply.

In what way, have you experienced the benefit of the glory of His presence?

Breaking Misery and Poverty

*but when we cried out to the **LORD**, he heard our **cry** and sent an angel...* (Numbers 20:16).

PERSISTENT misery and poverty have robbed many of their destiny and purpose in life. May this plague not come upon you. If you have experienced it, may it cease to exist in your life. God will put an end to misery, poverty, sorrow, and persistent lack of success in your life. Pray and proclaim along these lines: if it arises from your sins that God will say, *"Enough! Withdraw your hand"* (2 Sam. 24:16b). If it comes from the work of the devil, that God will say, *"The Lord rebuke you, Satan"* (Zech. 3:2).

Persistent misery and poverty is a debilitating condition, and you need to cry out to God! The widow of a certain prophet suffered this problem. Her husband though a prophet could not break free from this persistent misery, his goodness alone could not solve the problem; so when he died, he left his family to continue in the misery of poverty. But his widow cried out, *"My husband who served you is dead, and you know how he feared the Lord. But now a creditor has come, threatening to take my two sons as slaves"* (2 Kings 4:1 NLT).

She cried out—you must cry out too. The Lord will change your world from misery and poverty to gladness and wealth.

Are you suffering from persistent misery and poverty?

Growing in Christ

No, brothers, I am still not all I should be but I am bringing all my energies to bear on this one thing: Forgetting the past and looking forward to what lies ahead, I strain to reach the end of the race and receive the prize for which God is calling us up to heaven because of what Christ Jesus did for us (Philippians 3:13 Living Bible).

LIFE in Christ is a growing experience. You should never be too grown up that you think you have no more to learn. This was how the apostle Paul viewed the future, with joyful expectation of what lies ahead, what more there was to learn about Jesus Christ.

To Paul, life was a continuous learning process focused on Him who called him. What or who is teaching you? The value of today lies in the lessons of today.

I went past the field of a sluggard, past the vineyard of someone who has no sense; thorns had come up everywhere, the ground was covered with weeds, and the stone wall was in ruins. I applied my heart to what I observed and learned a lesson from what I saw (Proverbs 24:30-32).

Be blessed.

How many lessons have you learned today?

That the Living May Know

*This sentence is by the decree of the [heavenly] watch-ers and the decision is by the word of the holy ones, to the intent **that the living may know that the Most High [God] rules** the kingdom of mankind and gives it to whomever He will and sets over it the humblest and lowliest of men* (Daniel 4:17 AMP).

IT may not always seem that the Lord reigns, but know for sure that the Most High rules the earth and the heavens. The prophet Daniel made it very clear that we are to meditate on Him until the Morning Star dawns in your heart.

The Scriptures also say, *"Ascribe to the Lord the glory due His name...worship the Lord in the splendor of his holiness. Tremble before Him, all the earth! The world is firmly established; it cannot be moved. Let the heavens rejoice, let the earth be glad; let them say among the nations, "The Lord reigns!"* (1 Chron. 16:29-31).

How do you know God reigns?

Reading the Bible in a Year: Job 19-20 & Acts 9:23-43.

Your Time Is in His Hands

*But I trust in you, LORD; I say, "You are my God." **My times are in your hands;** deliver me from the hands of my enemies, from those who pursue me* (Psalm 31:14-15).

THIS verse in Psalm 31 is a palmist's realization and sweet surrender to the saving hands of God. God never fails! Indeed, His vision for you is for an appointed time.

This season is when Heaven will touch the earth for your sake like never before, establish the decrees of God over your life and over your family.

This is your time, your set time, and your season to reign with Him.

Do you acknowledge that God's timing is perfect?

The Time of Miracles and Victories

*He performs wonders that cannot be fathomed, **miracles** that cannot be counted* (Job 5:9).

THIS day, week, month, year is when you will mature and take dominion over evil. Threats of disorder and confusion will dissipate as you choose God over fleshly delights.

Now is when God will show you the difference between those who serve Him and those who serve Him not.

In God's good timing, He will:

- Crown your years with His bounty and your cart will overflow with abundance (Ps. 65:11).
- Make streams in the wasteland for you (Isa. 43:18-19).
- Give you blessings enough for three years (Lev. 25:21).
- Turn your valley of bacca (weeping) into a place of refreshing springs (Ps. 84:6) and your valley of anchor (troubles) into the door of hope (Hos. 2:13).

This is your time, this is your season to reign!

Are you ready for all good things to happen in God's good timing?

Put All Your Trust in Him

Blessed is the one who trusts in the LORD, who does not look to the proud, to those who turn aside to false gods (Psalm 40:4).

L ET these words resonate in your spirit; this is your time to take a stand for the Lord more than ever before. Take the necessary step of faith, He will not fail you. Whoever puts their trust in Him will never be disappointed.

Follow the Lord God with all your strength; *"How long will you waver between two opinions? If the Lord is God, follow Him"* (1 Kings 18:21). Apostle Paul said, *"But whatever were gains to me I now consider loss for the sake of Christ...that I may gain Christ"* (Phil. 3:7-8).

Also trust Him for the physical healing you require today, *"For I am the Lord who heals you"* (Exod. 15:26). Healing is the children's bread! You are healed and delivered when you put all your trust in Him.

Are you trusting Him for your healing, finances, marriage, relationships, career?

Testimony

*And this gospel of the kingdom will be preached in the whole world as a **testimony** to all nations, and then the end will come* (Matthew 24:14).

Testimonies are the attributes of God that were made manifest in our circumstances; so when the days of testimonies are upon us, it means God is strong on behalf of us in many ways.

*So do not be ashamed of the **testimony** about our Lord or of me his prisoner. Rather, join with me in suffering for the gospel, by the power of God* (2 Timothy 2:8).

Prophet Daniel said that the Revealer of mysteries revealed to him what the king wanted to know. The attribute of God to know all things and be able to share His secret with those who fear Him gave Daniel a testimony that saved his life.

May the Lord help you to appropriate it!

When is the last time you gave your testimony to another about His mercy and grace?

Number Your Days

*__Teach us to number our days__, that we may gain a
heart of wisdom* (Psalm 90:12).

M AKE each of your days count. The psalmist tells us to number
our days so we can have a heart of wisdom. A heart of wisdom
gives you power over the enemy—strength to face problems.

I pray that you never lose another day to the enemy of your soul!

May it be said of you as it was written of Isaac: *"Isaac...died...
being old and full of days"* (Gen. 35:29).

Your life will be full of joyful days when you walk in His ways!
May every one of your days count before God!

How can you make today count for Him?

Rejoice!

Rejoice in the Lord always. I will say it again: Rejoice! Let your gentleness be evident to all. The Lord is near. Do not be anxious about anything, but in every situation, by prayer and petition, with thanksgiving, present your requests to God. ...whatever is true, whatever is noble, whatever is right, whatever is pure, whatever is lovely, whatever is admirable—if anything is excellent or praiseworthy—think about such things. ...And the God of peace will be with you
(Philippians 4:4-9).

M AY your life be filled with joy and rejoicing be in your mouth and mind continually. When you take time to think about things that are right, pure, lovely, and admirable, your mindset becomes the same.

Destroy evil and hateful thoughts—replace them with things that are excellent and praiseworthy.

What brings a smile to your mind and face when you think about it?

Praying Together

PRAYING together or in unison has a penetrating capacity in the realm of the spirit. Concerning the promises of God in your life, unity in prayer and doing the following facilitates fruition:

1. Invite the power of the Holy Spirit into your life, *"The Holy Spirit will come upon you and the power of the Most High will overshadow you"* (Luke 1:35); and ask the Spirit of God to overwhelm you, *"The Spirit of the Lord will come powerfully upon you...and you will be changed into a different person"* (1 Sam. 10:6).

2. Pray that your steps will be ordered by God and that you will have the mind of Christ; *"Once these signs are fulfilled, do whatever your hand finds to do, for God is with you"* (1 Sam. 10:7).

3. For with God nothing shall be impossible; *"For every promise from God shall surely come true"* (Luke 1:37 Living Bible).

Are you comfortable praying with and for others?

The Power of Faith

*With this in mind, we constantly pray for you, that our God may make you worthy of his calling, and that **by his power he may bring to fruition your every desire** for goodness and your every deed prompted by **faith*** (2 Thessalonians 1:11).

*and into an inheritance that can never perish, spoil or fade. **This inheritance is kept in heaven for you, who through faith are shielded by God's power** until the coming of the salvation that is ready to be revealed in the last time...* (1 Peter 1:4-6).

CHOOSE this day to believe God and enjoy His power!

Are you enjoying His power to accomplish your goals?

The Eternal King

But the LORD is the true God; he is the living God, the eternal King. When he is angry, the earth trembles; the nations cannot endure his wrath. "Tell them this: 'These gods, who did not make the heavens and the earth, will perish from the earth and from under the heavens.'" But God made the earth by his power; he founded the world by his wisdom and stretched out the heavens by his understanding (Jeremiah 10:10-12).

THIS God is your God! He is not only a living God, He is your eternal King. He gets angry and then the earth trembles. Nations don't endure His anger.

Faith in His wisdom brings understanding. How can you ever hope to understand an omnipotent God? Only through the Holy Spirit who is with you in every way throughout every day.

Is God, the eternal King, sitting on the throne of your heart, mind, and spirit?

Encouraging Words

I waited patiently for the Lord; and he inclined unto me, and heard my cry. He brought me up also out of a horrible pit, out of the miry clay, and set my feet upon a rock, and established my goings. And He has put a new song in my mouth, even praise unto our God; many shall see it, and fear, and trust in the Lord (Psalm 40:1-3 KJV).

A MEN!

Our God is able to rescue us from the miry clay of problems and set our feet upon the solid rock of Christ, on a path of freedom and good health. *When my heart is overwhelmed, lead me to the rock that is higher than I am.*

What Scripture do you turn to for encouragement?

Resurrection Day

Jesus said to her, "I am the resurrection and the life. The one who believes in me will live, even though they die; and whoever lives by believing in me will never die. Do you believe this?"
(John 11:25-26).

JESUS was the perfect Passover Lamb; He died and was resurrected on the third day.

Passover is:

1. When evil and judgment passes over you and your household (see Exod. 12:1-30).

2. A household affair; a blessing for your family.

3. A meal eaten in haste, for divine acceleration to your promises.

4. The story told to all, including children, during the meal as a "now event"—a continuous thing; passing over to freedom and salvation just as it happened in the past.

5. Divine validation: it establishes Israel as the people of God; we are His people, the sheep of His pasture.

6. A feast and season of new life in God, of hope and a new beginning.

May the remembrance of the Passover and the power of His resurrection be with you.

Have you ever celebrated Passover with a friend, family, at church or temple?

The Water He Gives

"Whoever believes in Me...rivers of living water will flow from within them" (John 7:38).

JESUS told the woman at the well, *"Indeed, the water I give them will become in them a spring of water welling up to eternal life"* (John 4:14). Note that there is living water in you waiting to connect with the River of Life in the New Jerusalem:

> *Then the angel showed me **the river of water of life** as clear as crystal, flowing from the throne of God and the Lamb. ... On each side of the river stood the tree of life bearing fruits every month. And the leaves of the tree are for the healing of the nations. No longer will there be any curse...* (Revelation 22:1-3).

Healing and fruitfulness are in you and are yours—refresh yourself today in His living water.

Are you parched? When have you last reached into the flowing waters inside?

Fear and Prosperity

*Who, then, are those **who fear the LORD?** He will instruct them in the ways they should choose. They will **spend their days in prosperity,** and their descendants will inherit the land. The LORD confides in those who fear him; he makes his covenant known to them. My eyes are ever on the LORD, for only he will release my feet from the snare* (Psalm 25:12-15).

I believe that your prosperity is as strong as your fear of the Lord and prayer life is deep!

I believe that is why the psalmist was able to say that those who fear the Lord will spend their days in prosperity. Through prayer, God makes His covenant known to those who fear Him.

May you always maintain a healthy fear of the Lord; and may you always prosper—keeping your feet from the snare of the devil.

Does being fearful yet prosperous intrigue you?

Send Praise First

After the death of Joshua, the Israelites asked the Lord, "Which tribe should go first to attack the Canaanites?" The Lord answered, "Judah [praise], for I have given them victory over the land" (Judges 1:1-2 NLT).

A T a very difficult and trying time in the history of Israel, God asked them to send first the tribe of Judah (meaning praise). This was during days when judges ruled Israel.

Judah was not the firstborn of Jacob, but I believe that God sent them first because Judah means praise! When you praise God, you get your victory and move from expectation to anticipation because, *"of God's tender mercy, the morning light from Heaven is about to break upon us [you]"* (Luke 1:78 NLT).

Is praising God part of your daily routine?

Happy Easter Sunday

Early on Sunday morning, while it was still dark, Mary Mag-dalene came to the tomb and found that the stone had been rolled away from the entrance (John 20:1 NLT).

THE words that set Christians apart from other people groups was heard that morning from the angel at His tomb, *"He is not here; for He is risen as He said"* (Matt. 28:6 NKJV).

Humankind's last enemy was defeated, *"by his* [Jesus'] *death he might break the power of him who holds the power of death—that is, the devil—"* (Heb. 2:14). Jesus is the only One who can say, *"I am He who lives, and was dead, and behold, I am live for evermore. Amen. And I have the keys of Hades and of death"* (Rev. 1:18 NKJV).

The power of satanic prerogatives over the realm of the death is surrendered to Jesus. Victory is yours! This is the victory that over-comes the world! The Spirit that brought Jesus' dead body to life lives in you! It quickens your mortal body.

Are you claiming victory over death?

No More Crumbs

You do not have to eat crumbs from someone else's table. You can connect to the heavenly supply of resources. Consider the following:

1. Jacob asked for a supply line rather than a mere handout from Uncle Laban, and God gave the strategy; see Genesis 30:29-33.

2. Destiny restored; First Chronicles 4:9 says Jabez was tired of misery; he cried out to the God of Israel and was reconnected to his destiny. He requested: to be blessed; his territory enlarged; that God's hand be with him; to be kept from evil; that he would not cause others pain. God granted his request.

3. The value of a contrite heart—quick to realize a mistake, quick to repent, and quick to receive forgiveness. *"I had nearly lost my foothold"* (Ps. 73:1-2). Pray for the quickening of your spirit to realize what you must do to avoid falling.

4. Fatherly honor given and received; Elisha honored Elijah and that was his qualifications to double the number of Elijah's miracles; see 2 Kings 3:11; 2:12-15; 13:14.

Are you directly connected to Heaven's resources?

No More Crumbs,
Continued

5. The place of prophetic instructions to succeed; see Second Chronicles 26:4-5, even great King Uzziah needed Prophet Zechariah.

6. Prayers of the leaders empowers for success; in Exodus 17:10-14, as long as Moses' hands were lifted up to Heaven, Joshua prevailed against the Amalekites.

7. Breaking the siege so that heavenly supply may flow; see Second Kings 7:7.

8. Regaining the cutting edge of the anointing in order to be restored to destiny and purpose; see Second Kings 6:6. Regaining your cutting edge and your means of participation in the future; the axe head will float again.

9. God does not necessarily use human methods; see Second Kings 3:15-20. The miracle of rain without clouds or wind, but the trenches were full of water!

10. Favor for ease of increase; see Exodus 12:35-3. Plunder the Egyptians and put the items on the shoulders of your children—provision for you and for your future generation.

**How can you get reconnected to
Heaven's resources?**

Prevail in a Hostile Workplace

THE following prayer suggestions and Scripture passages, when read carefully and prayerfully considered, will give you strength and confidence to do the righteous thing in God's sight and within the workplace. Workplace means different things to different people. For some people, they put on a completely different character from what they are outside their workplace because of the hostility at the workplace. We should remember to show forth godly character and prevail in all situations.

Pray for repentance. Jeremiah 14:7-9; 21-22 – *Although our sins testify against us, do something, LORD, for the sake of your name. For we have often rebelled; we have sinned against you. You who are the hope of Israel, its Savior in times of distress, why are you like a stranger in the land, like a traveler who stays only a night? Why are you like a man taken by surprise, like a warrior powerless to save? You are among us, LORD, and we bear your name; do not forsake us! For the sake of your name do not despise us; do not dishonor your glorious throne. Remember your covenant with us and do not break it. Do any of the worthless idols of the nations bring rain? Do the skies themselves send down showers? No, it is you, LORD our God. Therefore our hope is in you, for you are the one who does all this.*

No matter our mistakes, we should be humble enough to ask for forgiveness and ask for God's enablement.

Pray for wisdom. Luke 21:15 – *for I will give you the right words and such wisdom that none of your opponents will be able to reply or refute you!*

Are the challenges you face in your workplace overwhelming or welcomed?

Prevail in a Hostile Workplace,
Continued

PRAY for God to frustrate the plans of the enemy. *"who foils the signs of false prophets and makes fools of diviners"* (Isa. 44:25a). The plans of the enemy shall not stand! *"If any nation (thing) comes to fight (trouble, harass intimidate) you, it will not be sent by Me. Therefore it will be routed, for I am on your side...no weapon turned against you shall succeed and you will have justice against every courtroom lie"* (Isa. 54:15-17 Living Bible). This is the sound of victory.

Pray knowing that your God is the only true God. *"But the Lord is the true God, He is the living God, the everlasting King"* (Jer. 10:10a NKJV). *"These gods, who did not make the heavens and the earth, will perish from the earth and from under the heavens. But God made the earth by his power; he founded the world by his wisdom and stretched out the heavens by his understanding"* (Jer. 10:11-12).

This God is our God—at home and in the workplace!

Have you been confiding in co-workers
or God about the situation?

Prevail in a Hostile Workplace,
Continued

PRAY **that power will change hands in your favor**. *"On the thirteenth day of the twelfth month, the month of Adar, the edict commanded by the king was to be carried out. On this day the enemies of the Jews had hoped to overpower them, but now the tables were turned and the Jews got the upper hand over those who hated them"* (Esther 9:1).

Pray that God will give up a nation as ransom for you. *"Since you are precious and honored in my sight, and because I love you, I will give people in exchange for you, nations in exchange for your life"* (Isa. 43:4).

Where possible, are you leaning on God and
not your own understanding?

Armed for Battle

It is God who arms me with strength and keeps my way secure
(Psalm 18:32).

You armed me with strength for battle; you humbled my adversaries before me. You made my enemies turn their backs in flight, and I destroyed my foes (Psalm 18:39-40).

MAY this be your testimony!

I pray that you will recognize your strength through Christ and that He will fight your battles. Your way is secure—God is guarding it with His angels and protecting it with His mighty power.

You will be secure, *because there is hope; you will look about you and* **take your rest in safety** (Job 11:18).

**With Him, are you ready to do battle,
and then to rest in safety?**

God Provides—Always

*Command those who are rich in this present world not to be arrogant nor to put their hope in wealth, which is so uncertain, but to **put their hope in God, who richly provides** us with everything for our enjoyment* (1 Timothy 6:17).

G OD provides heavenly supply and provision, just as He sent wind from Heaven to bring quail from the sea to the ground near the camp of the Israelites. Likewise, He will provide for us miraculously, *"Now the Lord sent a wind that brought quail from the sea and let them fall all around the camp. For miles in every direction there were quail flying about three feet above the ground. So the people went out and caught quail all that day and throughout the night and all the next day, too. No one gathered less than fifty bushels! They spread the quail all around the camp to dry"* (Num. 11:31-32 NLT).

God will send His wind against your enemy and all evil plans against you, *"He causes the vapors to ascend from the ends of the earth; He makes lightning for the rain; He brings the wind out of His treasuries"* (Ps. 135:7 NKJV). *"Though he is fruitful among his brethren, an east wind shall come; The wind of the LORD shall come up from the wilderness. Then his spring shall become dry, And his fountain shall be dried up. He shall plunder the treasury of every desirable prize"* (Hos. 13:15 NKJV).

Are you trusting God to provide for your every need?

God Provides Life

*The thief does not come except to steal, and to kill, and to destroy. I [Jesus] have come that they may have **life**, and that they may have it more **abundant**ly* (John 10:10).

GOD gives eternal life—that you will not die but live. *"The right hand of the LORD is exalted; The right hand of the LORD does valiantly. I shall not die, but live, And declare the works of the LORD"* (Ps. 118:16-17).

The covenant blood of Jesus Christ fights for us. *"Because of the covenant I made with you, sealed with blood I will free your prisoners from death in a waterless dungeon"* (Zech. 9:11 Living Bible).

The Ancient of Days arises on our behalf. *"As I watched, this horn was waging war against the holy people and defeating them, until the Ancient of Days came and pronounced judgment in favor of the holy people of the Most High, and the time came when they possessed the kingdom"* (Dan. 7:21-22).

How abundant is the life you are living?

Ask and You Shall Receive

*May we shout for joy when we hear of your victory and raise a victory banner in the name of our God. **May the Lord answer all your prayers*** (Psalm 20:5).

1. Proclaim God's Word against evil decrees and evil altars that may come against you. *"By the word of the LORD a man of God came from Judah to Bethel, as Jeroboam was standing by the altar to make an offering. By the word of the LORD he cried out against the altar: "Altar, altar! This is what the LORD says: 'A son named Josiah will be born to the house of David. On you he will sacrifice the priests of the high places who make offerings here, and human bones will be burned on you.'" That same day the man of God gave a sign: "This is the sign the LORD has declared: The altar will be split apart and the ashes on it will be poured out"* (1 Kings 13:1-3).

2. Ask for uncommon favor that, if necessary, the rules should be bent to favor you. *"But his father refused and said, 'I know, my son, I know. He too will become a people, and he too will become great. Nevertheless, his younger brother will be greater than he, and his descendants will become a group of nations.' He blessed them that day and said, 'In your name will Israel pronounce this blessing: "May God make you like Ephraim and Manasseh."' So he put Ephraim ahead of Manasseh"* (Gen. 48:19-20).

3. That the Lord should command blessing on you and your barn and that you will will rejoice knowing, *"The LORD will send a blessing on your barns and on everything you put your hand to. The LORD your God will bless you in the land he is giving you"* (Deut. 28:8).

When you pray, do you expect an answer from God?

Reading the Bible in a Year: Psalm 41-43 & Acts 24.

Defeating the Spirit of Procrastination

Direct my footsteps according to your word; let no sin rule over me (Psalm 119:133).

L IKE a cancerous worm, procrastination slowly eats away one's potential. Often it is hard to detect, but it dangerously and steadily devours the destinies of many people and lays waste much giftedness. It is an attitude that must be fought with all strength so it may not have root in you.

These are some of the ways to combat the menace: first, pray and confront the problem! Do not let the spirits of procrastination, defeat, regret have dominion over you. Pray that you prevail over the demonically inspired spirit of missed-appointments—opportunities that were lost as a result of demonic manipulations. Over time, this brings inertia and lack of zeal to a new day leading to procrastination.

Pray that in its place you will get divine appointments—opportunities pre or re-arranged by God. Pray also that those ordained to help you be willing and ready for you and there should be no more delay. Demonic delays bring frustration and down-sizing of one's vision or plans and ultimately to procrastination. "*The LORD says to my lord: "Sit at my right hand until I make your enemies a footstool for your feet." The LORD will extend your mighty sceptre from Zion, saying, "Rule in the midst of your enemies!"* (Ps. 110:1-2).

What can you do to never lose another day to the evil of the spirit of procrastination?

This for That

to proclaim the year of the LORD's favor and the day of vengeance of our God, to comfort all who mourn, and provide for those who grieve in Zion—to bestow on them a crown of beauty instead of ashes, the oil of joy instead of mourning, and a garment of praise instead of a spirit of despair. They will be called oaks of righteousness, a planting of the LORD for the display of his splendor. They will rebuild the ancient ruins and restore the places long devastated; they will renew the ruined cities that have been devastated for generations (Isaiah 61:2-4).

THIS is your season of restoration and divine exchange; ashes for beauty, mourning for gladness, and despair for a garment of praise that you will become the display of His splendor!

God is eager to exchange your sadness for joy, your suffering for healing, and your frown with a smile. His is most pleased when you are enjoying the life He blessed you with. May you always remember His goodness and faithfulness—even in times of this rather than that.

How abundant is the life you are living?

Breaking the Bond of Wickedness

*Is this not the **fast** that I have chosen: **To loose the bonds of wickedness,** to undo the heavy burdens, to let the oppressed go free, and that you break every yoke? Is it not to **share your bread** with the hungry, and that you **bring to your house the poor** who are cast out; when you see the naked, that you **cover him,** and not hide yourself from your own flesh? Then your light shall break forth like the morning, your healing shall spring forth speedily, and your righteousness shall go before you; the glory of the LORD shall be your rear guard* (Isaiah 58:6-8 NKJV).

Fasting and prayers break the bond of wickedness, among other things. When you show mercy and kindness to others (see above), you will be healed, your burdens will be lightened, your oppressor will flee.

This Scripture passage is full of ways you can loose the bonds of wickedness and break every aspect of bondage that restricts and limits your abilities, talents, and willingness to serve the Lord.

I pray that you will take to heart the admonitions and set a path toward having the Lord as your rear guard.

How many good works can you determine from Isaiah 58:6-8?

Your Living Hope

*Praise be to the God and Father of our Lord Jesus Christ! In his great mercy he has given us new birth into **a living hope** through the resurrection of Jesus Christ from the dead, and into an inheritance that can never perish, spoil or fade. This inheritance is kept in heaven for you* (1 Peter 1:3-4).

MAY the Lord send blessings on your work and on everything you put to hand to do! May you know the power of His resurrection in all that concerns you! Jesus has risen; the grave could not hold Him!

May the power of His resurrection be evident in all of your life!

How evident is His resurrection in your life?

The Blessings of Asher

...Most blessed of sons is Asher, let him be favored by his brothers and let him bathe his feet in oil (Deuteronomy 33:24).

T HE blessings of Asher are the blessing of dominance, supremacy, and of access to easy increase. Let this blessing come upon you. May you accept this blessing as the Lord desires.

Symbolically, the feet speak of the state of the heart and oil speaks of the anointing. To bathe your feet in oil is to allow the anointing of God into your heart and the anointing to cushion your walk on the hard terrain of life.

Are you hesitant about accepting blessings?

Keep Hope Alive

"Refrain your voice from weeping, and your eyes from tears; for your work shall be rewarded," says the LORD, "And they shall come back from the land of the enemy. **There is hope in your future***," says the LORD...* (Jeremiah 31:16-17).

THESE are the words of the prophet Jeremiah, but the restoration comes from the Rock of Ages—God Almighty.

Hope is the anchor for the future, and I believe the church is in the season of restoration from the Rock of Ages.

May this be your portion.

Is hope something you are full of, or lacking?

Prayer Makes All the Difference

Now it came to pass, as He was praying in a certain place, when He ceased, that one of His disciples said to Him, "Lord, teach us to pray, as John also taught his disciples." So He said to them, "When you pray, say: Our Father in heaven, hallowed be Your name. Your kingdom come. Your will be done on earth as it is in heaven. Give us day by day our daily bread. And forgive us our sins, for we also forgive everyone who is indebted to us. And do not lead us into temptation, but deliver us from the evil one" (Luke 11:1-4 NKJV).

PRAYERS will always make the difference. There is a growing need to pray as global uncertainty increases. More than ever before we need to pray! Paul prayed much, and he appreciated the prayers of others on his behalf, *"Yes, and I will continue to rejoice, for I know that through your prayers and God's provision of the Spirit of Jesus Christ what has happened to me will turn out for my deliverance"* (Phil. 1:18-19).

Your time has come and your prayers are being answered.

Do you daily pray the Lord's Prayer?

His Anointed

*Now this I know: **The LORD gives victory to his anointed.***
He answers him from his heavenly sanctuary with the victo-
rious power of his right hand (Psalm 20:6).

A NOINTING is the powerful expression of the Holy Spirit! Refer-
ring to the benefits of the anointing and the anointed the Bible
says, *"the Lord saves His anointed"* (Ps. 20:6). His anointing in your
life will preserve, provide, and empower you to your place of purpose!

Pray and faint not! For in due season you will reap your reward!
Let this truth abide in your spirit, *"I will now restore the fortunes of
Jacob and will have compassion on all the people,"* says God in Ezekiel
39:25. This will be your portion! Your fortunes will now be restored.

Do you accept freely His anointing on your life?

The Lord Saves

The LORD your God is with you, the Mighty Warrior who saves. He will take great delight in you; in his love he will no longer rebuke you, but will rejoice over you with singing (Zephaniah 3:17).

THIS is the day the Lord has made, and you have decided to rejoice and be glad in it!

This is what Jonathan said, *"Nothing can hinder the Lord from saving, whether by many or by few"* And the Living Bible adds, *"For it makes no difference to Him how many enemy troops there are!"* (1 Sam. 14:6).

The truth is, the battle belongs to the Lord!

The Lord will save you because you know that when you take refuge in Him, no one and no thing can harm you. *"The **LORD helps** them and **delivers** them; he delivers them from the wicked and **saves** them, because they take refuge in him"* (Ps. 37:40).

The Man of War will fight for you!

Are you standing beside God as He goes into battle for you?

The Breaker Anointing

THE Bible says. "The Breaker goes up before them; they break out, pass through the gate and go out by it" (Micah 2:13 NASB). The breaker is the Lord!

You will break out from a place of limitation to a place of destiny! The Lord will make a way! Pray that you will have divine acceleration even as He watches His Word in your life, *"The LORD said to me, "You have seen correctly, for I am watching to see that my word is fulfilled"* (Jer. 1:12). He is watching over His promise to fulfill it.

Pray that God will pull down anything that stops you from raising your head, *"What are these coming to do?" He answered, "These are the horns that scattered Judah so that no one could raise their head, but the craftsmen have come to terrify them and throw down these horns of the nations who lifted up their horns against the land of Judah to scatter its people"* (Zech. 1:21).

**Is your head raised high as you
break out into your place of destiny?**

God Decrees Justice

*Arise, LORD, in your anger; **rise up against the rage of my enemies.** Awake, my God; **decree justice** (Psalm 7:6).*

M AY the Lord rouse Himself as He did at Mount Perazim on your behalf!

*that it might be fulfilled which was spoken by Isaiah the prophet, saying:" Behold! My Servant whom I have chosen, My Beloved in whom My soul is well pleased! I will put My Spirit upon Him, And **He will declare justice**..." (Matthew 12:17-18).*

Let us say, *"It is time for You to act, Lord; your law is being broken,"* (Ps. 119:126).

Then suddenly the Lord will act on His promises in your behalf and what you have prayed about will come to pass (see Isa. 48:3).

Have you witnessed injustice?

Defeating the Spirit of Complacency

*When I whistle to them, **they will come running**"*
(Zechariah 10:8 Living Bible).

P LEASE pray the spirit of obedience to be poured out upon you and your family and for God to break any spirit of delay, procrastination, and lack of zeal—for then you all will be increased in many ways.

I will whistle for them and gather them, for I will redeem them; and they shall increase as they once increased (Zechariah 10:8).

I pray that you will realize the importance of responding to His calling immediately. Sometimes we miss His still small voice, but He is faithful to call again. Be ever vigil to lean your ear toward His whispers to you. Be also aware of His shouting!

How complacent are you when it comes to responding to God?

Remain Obedient

*Therefore, King Agrippa, **I was not disobedient to the heavenly vision,** but declared first to those in Damascus and in Jerusalem, and throughout all the region of Judea, and then to the Gentiles, that they should repent, turn to God, and do works befitting repentance* (Acts 26:19-20).

S TANDING before a powerful king who could decide whether he lives or not, Paul declared that he was *"not disobedient to the vision from heaven"* (Acts 26:19).

The most important thing: remain obedient to God no matter what and He, not man can perfect what concerns you!

You shall receive blessings from the Lord and righteousness from the God of your salvation! This is true of all those who seek the face of God (see Ps. 24:5-6).

May the Lord grant you double honor!

**Standing before others, will you declare
your obedience to God?**

Abigail's Prayer

"Please forgive your servant's presumption. The LORD your God will certainly make a lasting dynasty for my lord, because you fight the LORD's battles, and no wrongdoing will be found in you as long as you live. Even though someone is pursuing you to take your life, the life of my lord will be **bound securely in the bundle of the living by the LORD your God,** *but* **the lives of your enemies he will hurl away** *as from the pocket of a sling. When the LORD has fulfilled for my lord every good thing he promised concerning him and has appointed him ruler over Israel, my lord will not have on his conscience the staggering burden of needless bloodshed or of having avenged himself. And when the LORD your God has brought my lord success, remember your servant"* (1 Samuel 25:29).

THIS was Abigail's prayer for David, that his life will be, *"bound in the bundle of living"* and that his enemies will be *"hurled away."* She also wanted David not to have stain on his conscience. Her prayer was answered in ten days!

Let these prayers put you in a state of exception from judgment, including any form of judgmental suspension of the benefits of divine blessings in your life. From now on you are bound in the bundle of living!

How faithful are you to pray for others?

Ebenezer

But that day the Lord thundered with loud thunder against the Philistines and threw them into such a panic....Then Samuel took a stone and...named it Ebenezer, saying, "Thus far the LORD has helped us (1 Samuel 7:10-12).

MAY the Lord send panic to your enemies and may you testify saying, "Thus far the Lord has helped me."

One of the lasting legacies we can leave for the future generation is the story of how we have overcome enemies and adversities by the mercies of God. This was one of the memorial stones raised by the Israelites—Ebenezer—thus far the Lord has been faithful.

May the Lord grant you the cause to rejoice in Him.

Are you leaving a lasting legacy about His faithfulness to help you?

Your Personal Deliverer

LORD, you alone are my portion and my cup; you make my lot secure. The boundary lines have fallen for me in pleasant places; surely I have a delightful inheritance (Psalm 16:5-6).

B Y salvation and acceptance of Christ as your personal Savior, you are not only heavenly bound, your lot on earth became secured and every unpleasant issue and circumstance are to be cut off. From time to time, let your prayers include not only your own personal struggles or desires, but also those around you. Every eagle needs a push to a higher level, and today commit to pushing someone to a higher level.

Push your spouse, children, parents, colleagues to a higher vantage point! New oil for a new season! New level, new victory.

but those who hope in the LORD *will renew their strength. They will soar on wings like eagles; they will run and not grow weary, they will walk and not be faint* (Isaiah 40:31).

Declare also that the Lord will use your situation for your good and to further your service in His Kingdom agenda on earth.

Do you soar on eagles' wings?
Do you pray the same for others?

The Lord Appears

*The king went to Gibeon to offer sacrifices, for that was the most important high place, and Solomon offered a thousand burnt offerings on that altar. At Gibeon **the LORD appeared to Solomon** during the night in a dream, and God said, "Ask for whatever you want me to give you* (1 Kings 3:4-5).

K ING Solomon was renowned for extravagant worship; and in response, he was often blessed with awesome and glorious appearances of the Lord to him on personal level:

the LORD appeared to him a second time, as he had appeared to him at Gibeon (1 Kings 9:2).

May the Lord visit you as a person visits a friend.

Do you expect an appearance from the Lord, your eternal Friend?

Let Your Words Be Near to God

"And may these words of mine, which I have prayed before the LORD, **be near to the LORD our God day and night,** *that he may uphold the cause of his servant and the cause of his people Israel according to each day's need"* (1 Kings 8:59).

THESE are words from one of King Solomon's prayers that caused the release of the awesome glory of God from Heaven and filled the temple.

May your words never be far from your Lord God.

Have you wondered about how close your words are to God?

A TURNING POINT

*Then David sent messengers to get her. She came to him,
and he slept with her* (2 Samuel 11:4).

He [Solomon] *had seven hundred wives of royal birth and
three hundred concubines, and his wives led him astray*
(1 Kings 11:3).

CHAPTER 11 of Second Samuel was to King David as chapter 11 of First Kings was to King Solomon. In both of these chapters, both kings became victims of their uncontrolled sexual desires.

If the events of these chapters never happened, their stories would have been totally different. These were their turning points—the sexual detours in their otherwise outstanding rulerships. Their weakness to sexual sins took them in the wrong direction.

The wisdom of God is needed at turning-point situations.

May sexual sin not lead you down the wrong path.

Avoiding Intrigues

"Go to bed and pretend to be ill," Jonadab said. "When your father comes to see you, say to him, 'I would like my sister Tamar to come and give me something to eat. Let her prepare the food in my sight so I may watch her and then eat it from her hand'" (2 Samuel 13:5).

THERE are many people with the spirit of Jonadab—these are the characteristics of these people: very shrewd personality, prey on people with weakness, create tension, thrive on conflict, gossiping, befriend people in high places, and set people up for disasters.

But Jonadab son of Shimeah, David's brother, said, "My lord should not think that they killed all the princes; only Amnon is dead. This has been Absalom's express intention ever since the day Amnon raped his sister Tamar. My lord the king should not be concerned about the report that all the king's sons are dead. Only Amnon is dead." Meanwhile, Absalom had fled. Now the man standing watch looked up and saw many people on the road west of him, coming down the side of the hill. The watchman went and told the king, "I see men in the direction of Horonaim, on the side of the hill." Jonadab said to the king, "See, the king's sons have come; it has happened just as your servant said." As he finished speaking, the king's sons came in, wailing loudly. The king, too, and all his attendants wept very bitterly.

Do you know people who are possessed
by the spirit of Jonadad?

Warnings for Singles

*Now Dinah, the daughter Leah had borne to Jacob, went out
to visit the women of the land* [the city of Shechem]
(Genesis 34:1).

Dinah mingled with the wrong company and her lot in life was drastically altered. She was violated in the city of Shechem! The company you keep matters. The following few days focus on the special situations that affect people who are not married—although the truth revealed certainly applies to all people.

Control your lustfulness. *"In the course of time, Amnon son of David fell in love with Tamar, the beautiful sister of Absalom son of David. Amnon became so obsessed with his sister Tamar that he made himself ill. She was a virgin, and it seemed impossible for him to do anything to her"* (2 Sam. 13:1-2).

Beware of shrewd friends. *"Now Amnon had an adviser named Jonadab son of Shimeah, David's brother. Jonadab was a very shrewd man"* (2 Sam. 13:3).

Beware of people who pump you up all the time. Do not fall for the trap of flattery. *"For such people are not serving our Lord Christ, but their own appetites. By smooth talk and **flattery** they deceive the minds of naive people"* (Rom. 16:18).

Married or single, can you learn from these candid warnings?

Warnings for Singles,
Continued

...the devil...for he is a liar and the father of lies (John 8:44).

Notice warning signs or dangers. *"Then she took the pan and served him the bread, but he refused to eat. 'Send everyone out of here,' Amnon said. So everyone left him"* (2 Sam. 13:9).

Beware of suggestive actions or requests of impending or imminent promise. *"Then Amnon said to Tamar, 'Bring the food here into my bedroom so I may eat from your hand.' And Tamar took the bread she had prepared and brought it to her brother Amnon in his bedroom"* (2 Sam. 13:10).

Are you easily flattered and thereby put at risk?

Warnings for Singles,
Continued

For out of the heart come evil thoughts—murder, adultery, sexual immorality, theft, false testimony, slander (Matthew 15:19).

A**VOID** impulsive actions. *"But when she took it to him to eat, he grabbed her and said, "Come to bed with me, my sister"* (2 Sam. 13:11).

Don't negotiate with a sexually aroused man. The hormones are in control not the brain. When a man is aroused, there is no off-button. *"But he refused to listen to her, and since he was stronger than she, he raped her"* (2 Sam. 13:14).

Recognize the influence of hormones. After the hormones have died down, reality sets in. *"Then Amnon hated her with intense hatred. In fact, he hated her more than he had loved her. Amnon said to her, "Get up and get out!"* (2 Sam. 13:15).

Don't become damaged for life. *"He called his personal servant and said, "Get this woman out of my sight and bolt the door after her." So his servant put her out and bolted the door after her. She was wearing an ornate robe, for this was the kind of garment the virgin daughters of the king wore. Tamar put ashes on her head and tore the ornate robe she was wearing. She put her hands on her head and went away, weeping aloud as she went"* (2 Sam. 13:17-19).

**What feelings stirred within you when
you read of Tamar's rape?**

Warnings for Singles,
Continued

...turn your ear to my [God's] *words. Do not let them out of your sight, keep them within your heart; for they are life to those who find them and health to one's whole body. Above all else, guard your heart...* (Proverbs 4:20-23).

HOLD on to hope no matter the provocation or violation. Tamar gave herself no chance and listened to no advice. *"Tamar put ashes on her head and tore the ornate robe she was wearing. She put her hands on her head and went away, weeping aloud as she went"* (2 Sam. 13:19).

There is life after a misfortune. Tamar gave up on life. *"Her brother Absalom said to her, "Has that Amnon, your brother, been with you? Be quiet for now, my sister; he is your brother. Don't take this thing to heart." And Tamar lived in her brother Absalom's house, a desolate woman"* (2 Sam. 13:20).

Evil reaps what it sows. Amnon was killed by Absalom. *"Absalom ordered his men, "Listen! When Amnon is in high spirits from drinking wine and I say to you, 'Strike Amnon down,' then kill him. Don't be afraid. Haven't I given you this order? Be strong and brave." So Absalom's men did to Amnon what Absalom had ordered. Then all the king's sons got up, mounted their mules and fled"* (2 Sam. 13:28-29).

How easily do you recover from calamity, despair, disappointment, betrayal?

Nathan

David burned with anger against the man and said to Nathan, "As surely as the LORD lives, the man who did this must die! He must pay for that lamb four times over, because he did such a thing and had no pity." Then Nathan said to David, "You are the man! This is what the LORD, the God of Israel, says: 'I anointed you king over Israel, and I delivered you from the hand of Saul. I gave your master's house to you, and your master's wives into your arms. I gave you all Israel and Judah. And if all this had been too little, I would have given you even more. Why did you despise the word of the LORD by doing what is evil in his eyes? (2 Samuel 12:5-9)

A spire to be a man like Nathan. Nathan is a man worthy of emulation. He did outstanding things and handled extraordinary circumstances with godly fear and dexterity.

He was many things at different times: bold prophet, true prophet, political strategist, and obedient to God. When David was to build a temple for God, Nathan told David God's desires. Nathan had the courage to rebuke David about his affair with Bathsheba in a cleverly designed approach (see passage above). And Nathan was strategic in the defeat of Adonijah's plans. Nathan's move in this situation combined political strategy and obedience to the voice of God.

Is it time to look more deeply into the life of Nathan and learn some valuable lessons?

Intimacy with God

The boy Samuel ministered before the LORD under Eli. In those days the word of the LORD was rare; there were not many visions (1 Samuel 3:1).

THE life of Samuel as told in First Samuel 3 teaches us many things. These are attitudes we should imbibe in our walk with God. Samuel:

- Avoided the usual routines that did not line up with the godly order of things.
- Stayed in a place of responsibility.
- Was obedient at all times.
- Stayed with the ark of covenant, a place of His presence despite the corruption of the priest's sons around him.
- Showed remarkable willingness to serve God.
- Was keen to learn as he had a teachable spirit.

Then Eli realized that the LORD was calling the boy. So Eli told Samuel, "Go and lie down, and if he calls you, say, 'Speak, LORD, for your servant is listening.'" So Samuel went and lay down in his place. The LORD came and stood there, calling as at the other times, "Samuel! Samuel!" Then Samuel said, "Speak, for your servant is listening" (1 Samuel 3:8-10).

Are you listening for God's voice as young Samuel did?

Symbolism—the Language of the Spirit

When they went across the lake, the disciples forgot to take bread. "Be careful," Jesus said to them. "Be on your guard against the yeast of the Pharisees and Sadducees." They discussed this among themselves and said, "It is because we didn't bring any bread." Aware of their discussion, Jesus asked, "You of little faith, why are you talking among yourselves about having no bread? Do you still not understand? Don't you remember the five loaves for the five thousand, and how many basketfuls you gathered? Or the seven loaves for the four thousand, and how many basketfuls you gathered? How is it you don't understand that I was not talking to you about bread? But be on your guard against the yeast of the Pharisees and Sadducees." Then they understood that he was not telling them to guard against the yeast used in bread, but against the teaching of the Pharisees and Sadducees (Matthew 16:5-12).

GOD requires you not only to hear His voice but to understand what He says to you. That is why Jesus taught His disciples to understand the language of symbolism. The language of symbolism is the language of the Spirit.

Note that a symbol can mean different things at different times; for example, Jesus referred to yeast as something evil when He said, "beware of the yeast of the Pharisees" meaning the capacity of the wrong doctrine to spread. But He also referred to yeast as the symbol of the Kingdom of God, meaning the ability of the Kingdom to penetrate the world. The meaning of symbols should be derived for each occasion.

Do you understand the language of symbolism?

The Supernatural

Then Solomon awoke—and he realized it had been a dream. He returned to Jerusalem, stood before the ark of the Lord's covenant and sacrificed burnt offerings and fellowship offerings. Then he gave a feast for all his court (1 Kings 3:15).

WHATEVER experiences you have in life should be Bible-guided and in line with the principles of the Word of God. Your experiences can vary between two ends of the supernatural spectrum.

King Solomon (see passage above) awoke and realized he had a dream. For him, it felt so real as if it happened in the natural realm but it was supernatural occurrence.

"Peter followed him out of the prison, but he had no idea that what the angel was doing was really happening; he thought he was seeing a vision. ...suddenly the angel left him. Then Peter came to himself and said, "Now I know without a doubt that the Lord has sent his angel and rescued me from Herod's clutches and from everything the Jewish people were hoping would happen" (Acts 12:9-11). Peter "came to himself." It happened in the natural, but Peter thought it was happening in the realm of the supernatural.

These two examples illustrate that people can move in the borders of the supernatural and the natural realm. Both experiences show powerful moves of God. Expect God in both ways.

Have you witnessed or been part of any supernatural experiences?

A Privilege

*The **LORD appeared** to Abram and said, "To your offspring I will give this land." So he built an altar there to the LORD, who had appeared to him* (Genesis 12:7).

*Then Ananias went to the house and entered it. Placing his hands on Saul, he said, "Brother Saul, **the Lord—Jesus, who appeared to you** on the road as you were coming here—has sent me so that you may see again and be filled with the Holy Spirit"* (Acts 9:17).

WHAT a special privilege. I feel a holy desire for greater things in God whenever I read such kinds of privilege of frequent visitation and blessings by the Almighty God to a mere person.

Solomon enjoyed such privilege, and you can aspire to have this as well, *"the LORD appeared to him a second time, as he had appeared to him at Gibeon"* (1 Kings 9:2).

What was the secret of Solomon, Abraham, and Paul? They knew how to give God extravagant and unreserved worship. You, too, can be visited by the Creator of Heaven and earth.

Have you been worshiping your almighty God extravagantly, without reservation?

Never Take God for Granted

Although he had forbidden Solomon to follow other gods, Solomon did not keep the LORD's command. So the LORD said to Solomon, "Since this is your attitude and you have not kept my covenant and my decrees, which I commanded you, I will most certainly tear the kingdom away from you and give it to one of your subordinates (1 Kings 11:10-11).

EVERY now and again we all fall into the pattern of taking God for granted. But what is important is that once realized, we should take all necessary measures to reverse the tendency or spiritual drifting away from His principles.

Solomon and Eli's sons forfeited their privileges because of disobedience; they took their privilege for granted (see passage above). May you never take God's privilege or grace for granted.

Therefore the LORD, the God of Israel, declares: "I promised that members of your family would minister before me forever." But now the LORD declares: "Far be it from me! Those who honor me I will honor, but those who despise me will be disdained. The time is coming when I will cut short your strength and the strength of your priestly house, so that no one in it will reach old age" (1 Samuel 2:30-31).

Have you been taking God's blessing for granted?

Keeping God on Your Side

Then the LORD raised up against Solomon an adversary, Hadad the Edomite, from the royal line of Edom. And God raised up against Solomon another adversary, Rezon son of Eliada, who had fled from his master, Hadadezer king of Zobah. Rezon was Israel's adversary as long as Solomon lived, adding to the trouble caused by Hadad. So Rezon ruled in Aram and was hostile toward Israel. Also, Jeroboam son of Nebat rebelled against the king. He was one of Solomon's officials, an Ephraimite from Zeredah, and his mother was a widow named Zeruah (1 Kings 11:14,23,25-26).

THIS is the story of Solomon's downfall. King Solomon fell when God was no longer on his side. If God be for you, who can be against you; conversely, if God be against you, who can rescue you!

Let God fight *for* you and not against you.

**How careful are you about
keeping God as your ally?**

A Vessel of Dishonor in God's Hands

This is what the LORD says: "Do not go up to fight against your brothers, the Israelites. Go home, every one of you, for this is my doing" (1 Kings 12:23).

THIS is one of my fervent prayers, that God will not only continue to use you but that you will always be a vessel of honor in His hand. Never pray for God to use you without specifying how you would like Him to use you; remember, He uses the wicked even for His purpose. Here are some unusual turns of events that came from God and the lessons thereof:

1. Rehoboam, Solomon's son, made a foolish decision; as a consequence there was a turn of events from God (see 1 Kings 12:22-24).

2. Saul disobeyed God and God sent an evil spirit to torment him, an evil spirit was used for His purpose in this case to bring judgment on disobedient Saul. *"Now the Spirit of the LORD had departed from Saul, and an evil spirit from the LORD tormented him* (1 Sam. 16:14).

3. Samson's lust after Philistine women was used by God as an instrument to confront the Philistines. *"His father and mother replied, "Isn't there an acceptable woman among your relatives or among all our people? Must you go to the uncircumcised Philistines to get a wife?" But Samson said to his father, "Get her for me. She's the right one for me."* **His parents did not know that this was from the LORD,** *who was seeking an occasion to confront the Philistines; for at that time they were ruling over Israel.)* (Judg. 14:3-4).

How can you be sure that you are being used by God?

A Vessel of Dishonor in God's Hands, Continued

4. Hadad, the Edomite was used as a vessel in the hand of God against King Solomon. *"Then the LORD raised up against Solomon an adversary, Hadad the Edomite, from the royal line of Edom* (1 Kings 11:14).

5. Rezon of Aram was used as instrument to trouble the king of Israel, King Solomon. *"Rezon was Israel's adversary as long as Solomon lived, adding to the trouble caused by Hadad. So Rezon ruled in Aram and was hostile toward Israel* (1 Kings 11:25).

6. Ahab was lured to his death by a lying spirit from the throne of God. *Micaiah continued, "Therefore hear the word of the LORD: I saw the LORD sitting on his throne with all the multitudes of heaven standing on his right and on his left. And the LORD said, 'Who will entice Ahab king of Israel into attacking Ramoth Gilead and going to his death there?' One suggested this, and another that. Finally, a spirit came forward, stood before the LORD and said, 'I will entice him.' 'By what means?' the LORD asked. 'I will go and be a deceiving spirit in the mouths of all his prophets,' he said. 'You will succeed in enticing him,' said the LORD. 'Go and do it'* (2 Chron. 18:18-21).

How do you want God to use you?

The Falsehoods of Jeroboam

Jeroboam thought to himself, "The kingdom will now likely revert to the house of David. If these people go up to offer sacrifices at the temple of the LORD in Jerusalem, they will again give their allegiance to their lord, Rehoboam king of Judah. They will kill me and return to King Rehoboam." After seeking advice, the king made two golden calves. He said to the people, "It is too much for you to go up to Jerusalem. Here are your gods, Israel, who brought you up out of Egypt." ... Jeroboam built shrines on high places and appointed priests from all sorts of people, even though they were not Levites. He...offered sacrifices on the altar. ...he offered sacrifices on the altar he had built at Bethel. So he instituted the festival for the Israelites and went up to the altar to make offerings (1 Kings 12:26-33).

PERHAPS Jeroboam somehow justified the actions he took in his mind. Very likely he thought self-exaltation was better than serving God. Jeroboam did not repent, and God said, *"You have done more evil than all who lived before you. You have made for yourself other gods, idols made of metal; you have aroused my anger and turned your back on me"* (1 Kings 14:9).

Falsehoods are not uncommon, pray that God will help you avoid falsehoods in whatever form they may come.

Can you detect a falsehood quickly?

The Stale Prophet

*Then the LORD said to me, "The **prophets are prophesying lies** in my name. I have not sent them or appointed them or spoken to them. **They are prophesying to you false visions, divinations, idolatries and the delusions of their own minds*** (Jeremiah 14:14).

Have you ever experienced the deception of stale prophet? They are dead in giving council or receiving counsel from God. They recycle old revelations and manipulate people and circumstances.

Avoid them.

Here are things to look out for: no freshness, caught up worldly things, no evidence of signs of God, lacking in communion with God, using worldly strategy to maintain his role or office, receives scanty revelation, and is full of intrigues.

How susceptible are you to being deceived?

The Peculiar Blessing of Jeroboam

As for you, go back home. When you set foot in your city, the boy will die. All Israel will mourn for him and bury him. He is the only one belonging to Jeroboam who will be buried, because he is the only one in the house of Jeroboam in whom the LORD, the God of Israel, has found anything good (1 Kings 14:12-13).

H AVE you ever experienced a misfortune but it turned out later to be a blessing? The son of Jeroboam's death was a blessing from God! He died because God found something good in him. This was done in order that he alone averted the curse on Jeroboam's bloodline.

Think of another instance; God said those who were taken into Babylonian captivity were chosen remnants who would be remembered by God!

**Are you willing to look for the good
in your misfortunes?**

Reading the Bible in a Year: Psalm 139-141 & 1 Corinthians 10:1-13.

You Can Overcome Evil

When an impure spirit comes out of a person, it goes through arid places seeking rest and does not find it. Then it says, "I will return to the house I left." When it arrives, it finds the house unoccupied, swept clean and put in order. Then it goes and takes with it seven other spirits more wicked than itself, and they go in and live there. And the final condition of that person is worse than the first. That is how it will be with this wicked generation (Matthew 12:43-45).

O NLY in God can you overcome satan! Never on your own might. One of the reasons he often succeeds against believers is not only because he is not flesh and blood, but he sits at the apex of well-organized evil forces.

Jesus said if He cast out demons by demonic forces, then satan is divided among himself and he would not stand (see Luke 11:17-18). But he still exists today because he has a well-organized set-up.

The Bible also says when evil spirits are cast out, they go about looking for a new abode, finding none they come back to its previous place and they find the house clean, they go and get seven more (see passage above).

You and God can get the enemy on the run. There are levels of victory that you can only attain when you are united with Him; and many times, with other believers.

When you clean out your inner house, are you leaving it empty or filling it up with God's Word?

Discerning Sounds in the Spirit

But solid food belongs to those who are of full age, that is,
those who by reason of use have their senses exercised to dis-
cern both good and evil (Hebrews 5:14 NKJV).

L IKE the Book of Hebrews admonishes us, we should train our senses to discern what sound is emanating from the unseen realm of the spirit. What sounds are you hearing in the situations that surround you?

In the Book of Acts, the apostles in the upper room heard the sound of a mighty rushing wind, and the Bible described it as a sound from Heaven. *"When the day of Pentecost came, they were all together in one place. Suddenly a sound like the blowing of a violent wind came from heaven and filled the whole house where they were sitting"* (Acts 2:1-2). They knew it was not an ordinary sound.

In the Book of First Kings, the prophet Elijah spoken of the sound of abundance of rain, that will bring an end the famine; *"And Elijah said to Ahab, "Go, eat and drink, for there is the sound of a heavy rain"* (1 Kings 18:41).

How good are you at discerning
sounds in the Spirit?

Discerning Sounds in the Spirit,
Continued

*Then the man and his wife **heard the sound of the LORD
God** as he was walking in the garden in the cool of the day,
and they hid from the LORD God among the trees of the garden. But the LORD God called to the man, "Where are you?"*
(Genesis 3:8-9).

IN the Garden of Eden, Adam and Eve discerned the approach of
God even before they actually heard His voice. They heard the
sound of God's approach.

Moses and Joshua heard an unusual sound as they approached
the camp. It was not the sound of war, it was not the sound of victory;
it was the sound of the revelry, the sound of idol worshiping, *"When
Joshua heard the noise of the people shouting, he said to Moses, "There
is the sound of war in the camp." Moses replied, "It is not the sound
of victory it is not the sound of defeat; it is the sound of singing that I
hear"* (Exod. 32:17-18).

Train yourself to hear sounds in the spirit.

What sounds are you hearing right now?

The Life and Death and Life Lazarus

"Father, I thank you that you have heard me. I knew that you always hear me, but I said this for the benefit of the people standing here, that they may believe that you sent me." When he had said this, Jesus called in a loud voice, "Lazarus, come out!" (John 11:40-43).

THE following truths are worthy of examination and contemplation:

1. Before the death of Lazarus, there was a relationship between his sisters and Jesus. Relationship is the basis for demand and service in His vineyard.

2. Release is important. Release everything to God. When you have done all you can, release it to God. Such release is like rolling the stone away from the mouth of Lazarus's grave.

3. Martha got a revelation, that is why she was able to say "even now." It is never too late for God; life's Author.

4. Quitting temporarily removes the pain and amounts to suspension of expectation; quitting can bring false peace or unfounded security that crumbles as the dust settles. Don't quit, winners don't quit!

5. Restoration must be preceded with action of faith—like rolling the stone away. Take off human limitation, don't limit the Holy One of Israel. God can return what was taken from you.

What have you learned from these truths?

Admonitions and Commendations

Brothers and sisters, if someone is caught in a sin, you who live by the Spirit should restore that person gently. But watch yourselves, or you also may be tempted (Galatians 6:1).

Let us not become weary in doing good, for at the proper time we will reap a harvest if we do not give up (Galatians 6:9).

It is for freedom that Christ has set us free. Stand firm, then, and do not let yourselves be burdened again by a yoke of slavery (Galatians 5:1).

W HEN you come across admonitions and commendations in the Bible, take them seriously. As with the three passages from Galatians, there is light and love within His Word.

When you obey His Word and enjoy the fruit of His promises, may you always remember His faithfulness and return again and again to the wisdom He shares with you through the living Word.

Do you take admonitions and commendations seriously—enough?

Admonitions and Commendations,
Continued

*But I did not believe these things until I came and saw with
my own eyes. Indeed, not even half was told me; in wisdom
and wealth you have far exceeded the report I heard*
(1 Kings 10:7).

*I do not set aside the grace of God, for if righteousness could
be gained through the law, Christ died for nothing!*
(Galatians 2:21)

*Are you so foolish? After beginning by means of the Spirit,
are you now trying to finish by means of the flesh? Have you
experienced so much in vain—if it really was in vain? So
again I ask, does God give you his Spirit and work miracles
among you by the works of the law, or by your believing
what you heard? So also Abraham "believed God, and it
was credited to him as righteousness"* (Galatians 3:3-6).

Do you have to see with your own eyes what the Lord is telling
you, or are you willing to accept in faith? Do you believe that
righteousness can be gained through the law or by works? Have you
tried to finish God's work with your own power, or do you believe
that God has given you His Spirit, which works on your behalf?

Have you hidden these words in your heart?

Reading the Bible in a Year: Proverbs 5-6 & 1 Corinthians 14:1-20.

Admonitions and Commendations,
Continued

...The only thing that counts is faith expressing itself through love (Galatians 5:6).

...You were running a good race. Who cut in on you to keep you from obeying the truth? (Galatians 5:7).

I am confident in the Lord that you will take no other view. The one who is throwing you into confusion, whoever that may be, will have to pay the penalty (Galatians 5:10).

He was a good man, full of the Holy Spirit and faith, and a great number of people were brought to the Lord (Acts 11:24).

MAY you always combine faith and love while you are running the good race for Him. I pray that you will not be overwhelmed with the spirit of confusion and that you will be filled with the Holy Spirit, bringing many to salvation.

Are you running a good race?
Are you running to win?

The Miracle of Divine Provision

Then the word of the LORD came to Elijah: "Leave here, turn eastward and hide in the Kerith Ravine, east of the Jordan. You will drink from the brook, and I have directed the ravens to supply you with food there." So he did what the LORD had told him. He went to the Kerith Ravine, east of the Jordan, and stayed there. The ravens brought him bread and meat in the morning and bread and meat in the evening, and he drank from the brook (1 Kings 17:2-6).

T HE miracle of divine provision is God providing for us even when His way of doing so runs contrary to set patterns of human expectation or methods of operation. To experience the miracle of divine provision, let us, for the next few days, intimate ourselves with the ways He miraculously provided for others throughout the Scriptures.

The feeding of Elijah at the brook of Kerith by ravens is an outstanding miracle because ravens are dirty and selfish birds—but they provided clean meat for Elijah.

Has God provided food for you miraculously?

The Miracle of Divine Provision,
Continued

After Jesus and his disciples arrived in Capernaum, the collectors of the two-drachma temple tax came to Peter and asked, "Doesn't your teacher pay the temple tax?" "Yes, he does," he replied. When Peter came into the house, Jesus was the first to speak. "What do you think, Simon?" he asked. "From whom do the kings of the earth collect duty and taxes—from their own children or from others?" "From others," Peter answered. "Then the children are exempt," Jesus said to him. "But so that we may not cause offense, go to the lake and throw out your line. Take the first fish you catch; open its mouth and you will find a four-drachma coin. Take it and give it to them for my tax and yours (Matthew 17:24-27).

THE story of the fish with money in its mouth for the temple tax is not only amazing, but shows the supernatural way of God. Not only was money in the mouth of the fish, but it was caught by throwing a line to the fish, which was caught in the mouth yet the money did not drop out.

Has God provided finances for you miraculously?

The Miracle of Divine Provision,
Continued

For this is what the LORD says: You will see neither wind nor rain, yet this valley will be filled with water, and you, your cattle and your other animals will drink. This is an easy thing in the eyes of the LORD; he will also deliver Moab into your hands. You will overthrow every fortified city and every major town. You will cut down every good tree, stop up all the springs, and ruin every good field with stones." The next morning, about the time for offering the sacrifice, there it was—water flowing from the direction of Edom! And the land was filled with water (2 Kings 3:17-20).

H IS ways are not our ways and they are higher than our ways, we expect clouds, wind, then the rain before the pools of water may gather! But God can fill the trenches with water and gather pools of water without even a cloud, winds, or rain!

Has God provided refreshment for you miraculously?

The Miracle of Divine Provision,
Continued

Now there were four men with leprosy at the entrance of the city gate. They said to each other, "Why stay here until we die?... At dusk they got up and went to the camp of the Arameans. When they reached the edge of the camp, no one was there, for the Lord had caused the Arameans to hear the sound of chariots and horses and a great army, so that they said to one another, "Look, the king of Israel has hired the Hittite and Egyptian kings to attack us!" So they got up and fled in the dusk and abandoned their tents and their horses and donkeys. They left the camp as it was and ran for their lives. The men who had leprosy reached the edge of the camp, entered one of the tents and ate and drank. ..."We went into the Aramean camp and no one was there—not a sound of anyone—only tethered horses and donkeys, and the tents left just as they were." ...So they selected two chariots with their horses, and the king sent them after the Aramean army. He commanded the drivers, "Go and find out what has happened." ...Then the people went out and plundered the camp of the Arameans. So a seah of the finest flour sold for a shekel, and two seahs of barley sold for a shekel, as the LORD had said. ...The officer had said to the man of God, "Look, even if the LORD should open the floodgates of the heavens, could this happen?" The man of God had replied, "You will see it with your own eyes, but you will not eat any of it!" And that is exactly what happened to him... (2 Kings 7:3-20).

Gop can use the loneliest or the most despised person to achieve His goal. This is the story of the turnaround for four leprous men who marched out and brought the famine to an end.

Has God provided a miraculous way out?

The Miracle of Divine Provision,
Continued

A man came from Baal Shalishah, bringing the man of God twenty loaves of barley bread baked from the first ripe grain, along with some heads of new grain. "Give it to the people to eat," Elisha said. "How can I set this before a hundred men?" his servant asked. But Elisha answered, "Give it to the people to eat. For this is what the LORD says: 'They will eat and have some left over.'" Then he set it before them, and they ate and had some left over, according to the word of the LORD (2 Kings 4:42-44).

GOD can use the little you have to achieve the mighty purpose He has for you. God was the One who enabled Elijah to feed 100 people with so little. What He has done for one, He can do for another.

Has God provided resources for you miraculously?

The Miracle of Divine Provision,
Continued

One day as Jesus was standing by the Lake of Gennesaret, the people were crowding around him and listening to the word of God. He saw at the water's edge two boats, left there by the fishermen, who were washing their nets. He got into one of the boats, the one belonging to Simon, and asked him to put out a little from shore. Then he sat down and taught the people from the boat. When he had finished speaking, he said to Simon, "Put out into deep water, and let down the nets for a catch." ...When they had done so, they caught such a large number of fish that their nets began to break. ...When Simon Peter saw this, he fell at Jesus' knees and said, "Go away from me, Lord; I am a sinful man!" (Luke 5:1-8)

THE fishermen toiled all night and caught no fish. They were experienced and trained, and everyone knows that fish are caught at night. Humanly speaking they had done what ought to be done and were in the right place and at the right time—yet they caught no fish. Then the Lord gave the word to reach out to the deep even in the daytime and their story changed to that of a bountiful harvest of fish!

**Has God provided a career boost
for you miraculously?**

The Miracle of Divine Provision,
Continued

Some time later the brook dried up because there had been no rain in the land. Then the word of the LORD came to him: "Go at once to Zarephath in the region of Sidon and stay there. I have directed a widow there to supply you with food." ..."As surely as the LORD your God lives," she replied, "I don't have any bread—only a handful of flour in a jar and a little olive oil in a jug. I am gathering a few sticks to take home and make a meal for myself and my son, that we may eat it—and die." Elijah said to her, "Don't be afraid. ...For this is what the LORD, the God of Israel, says: 'The jar of flour will not be used up and the jug of oil will not run dry until the day the LORD sends rain on the land.'" She went away and did as Elijah had told her. So there was food every day for Elijah and for the woman and her family (1 Kings 17:7-15).

For Elijah, Zarepheth was the home of his enemy, and a widow is the most unlikely person to provide for anyone even at the best of times, and at the time there was a severe famine. So this was, therefore, a compounded impossibility. The story of the widow at Zarephath exemplifies the fact that God can use the most unusual means to provide for His people.

Has God provided a miracle for you though someone else?

The Miracle of Divine Provision,
Continued

The wife of a man from the company of the prophets cried out to Elisha, "Your servant my husband is dead, and you know that he revered the LORD. But now his creditor is coming to take my two boys as his slaves." Elisha replied to her, "How can I help you? Tell me, what do you have in your house?" "Your servant has nothing there at all," she said, "except a small jar of olive oil." Elisha said, "Go around and ask all your neighbors for empty jars. Don't ask for just a few. Then go inside and shut the door behind you and your sons. Pour oil into all the jars, and as each is filled, put it to one side." She left him and shut the door behind her and her sons. They brought the jars to her and she kept pouring. When all the jars were full, she said to her son, "Bring me another one." But he replied, "There is not a jar left." Then the oil stopped flowing. She went and told the man of God, and he said, "Go, sell the oil and pay your debts. You and your sons can live on what is left" (2 Kings 4:1-7).

G OD turned the little oil in the hand of the widow into abundance and broke the family line of poverty. She cried to God through the man of God. For some reason, her husband, though a good man, never cried out despite the burden of debts that he eventually left behind.

**Has God provided a miracle for you
to pay your debts?**

Turning Things Around

They went across the lake to the region of the Gerasenes. When Jesus got out of the boat, a man with an impure spirit came from the tombs to meet him. This man lived in the tombs, and no one could bind him anymore, not even with a chain. For he had often been chained hand and foot, but he tore the chains apart and broke the irons on his feet. No one was strong enough to subdue him. Night and day among the tombs and in the hills he would cry out and cut himself with stones. **When he saw Jesus from a distance, he ran and fell on his knees in front of him.** *He shouted at the top of his voice, "What do you want with me, Jesus, Son of the Most High God? In God's name don't torture me!" For Jesus had said to him, "Come out of this man, you impure spirit!" Then Jesus asked him, "What is your name?" "My name is Legion," he replied, "for we are many." ...The herd, about two thousand in number, rushed down the steep bank into the lake and were drowned. Those tending the pigs ran off and reported this in the town and countryside, and the people went out to see what had happened. ...As Jesus was getting into the boat, the man who had been demon-possessed begged to go with him. Jesus did not let him, but said, "Go home to your own people and tell them how much the Lord has done for you, and how he has had mercy on you"* (Mark 5:1-20).

THE demoniac of Gerasenes was a man no human being could help. Chains could not hold him, and he was a danger to himself and society. Yet when Jesus came his way, he cried out and "fell on his knees in front of Him." The result: he was delivered from his insanity.

Has God provided a miracle that set your mind at ease?

Reading the Bible in a Year: Proverbs 25-27 & 2 Corinthians 6.

Turning Things Around,
Continued

But now here are men from Ammon, Moab and Mount Seir, whose territory you would not allow Israel to invade when they came from Egypt; so they turned away from them and did not destroy them. See how they are repaying us by coming to drive us out of the possession you gave us as an inheritance. Our God, will you not judge them? For we have no power to face this vast army that is attacking us. We do not know what to do, but our eyes are on you.
(2 Chronicles 20:10-12).

HERE are people who decided to turn things around and make a difference in their lives. You can learn from their example. In their most hopeless situation, when faced by far superior forces, their fate humanly speaking was certain—destruction!

They cried out to God who is able stop anyone from falling, and they said, "Our eyes are on you, God; we do not know what to do."

God helped them and can do same for you today.

**What steps can you take today to
start turning things around in your life?**

Ancient Hostility

He will be a wild donkey of a man; his hand will be against everyone and everyone's hand against him, and he will live in hostility toward all his brothers (Genesis 16:12).

Now you, brothers and sisters, like Isaac, are children of promise. At that time the son born according to the flesh persecuted the son born by the power of the Spirit. It is the same now. But what does Scripture say? "Get rid of the slave woman and her son, for the slave woman's son will never share in the inheritance with the free woman's son." Therefore, brothers and sisters, we are not children of the slave woman, but of the free woman (Galatians 4:28-31).

THE mark of Ishmael has been seen and felt through the centuries. May you do your part to ease the hostility, to bring peace where there is none.

When within your power, do you bring peace or turmoil to situations?

Lack of Commitment

Then the LORD said to Moses, "Leave this place, you and the people you brought up out of Egypt, and go up to the land I promised on oath to Abraham, Isaac and Jacob, saying, 'I will give it to your descendants'" (Exodus 33:1).

THE Israelites' exodus from Egypt to the Promised Land is the story of a three-day journey that became a 40-year journey because of lack of commitment. Here are just a few of the things God did for the Israelites that should have ensured their commitment to Him:

1. God loaded them with gold and silver.
2. God performed some awesome miracles.
3. God divided the Red Sea.
4. God brought water out of the rock.
5. God changed bitter water to sweet water: yet they craved garlic and onion.

Despite all that the Lord did for the Israelites, they lacked purpose, so they had no faith in God's ability. They forgot that the power of God that brought them out of bondage was sufficient to take them into the Promised Land.

Have you forgotten all that God has done for you in the past?

Commitment to His Word

He [Jesus] *replied, "My mother and brothers are those who hear God's word and put it into practice"* (Luke 8:21).

COMMITMENT to God requires taking responsibilities seriously, including: a life of prayer, reading the Word of God, giving tithes, fasting, feeding your spirit.

Faith comes by the Word, Jesus defeated satan in the desert by declaring that man must not live by bread only, *"Jesus answered, 'It is written: "Man shall not live on bread alone, but on every word that comes from the mouth of God"'"* (Matt. 4:4). *"And without faith it is impossible to please God, because anyone who comes to him must believe that he exists and that he rewards those who earnestly seek him"* (Heb. 11:6). *"Heaven and earth will pass away but my words will never pass away"* (Mark 13:31).

When you spend time with God and in His Word, you stop complaining, gossiping, worrying, and all the other fleshly attributes of a person who isn't trusting God.

How committed are you to reading and meditating on His Word, the bread of life?

Lessons of Gilgal

Because of all their wickedness in Gilgal, I hated them there. Because of their sinful deeds, I will drive them out of my house. I will no longer love them; all their leaders are rebellious (Hosea 9:15).

GILGAL was the center of prophetic activity that looked to Elijah for leadership. But, Gilgal, by turn of fate, later became the center of pagan idolatry. How sad when things change for the worse rather than the better. When moral, ethical, and spiritual standards corrode, evil can easily slip in.

Here are some the statements that were later made of Gilgal:

- *Though you, Israel, commit adultery, do not let Judah become guilty. "Do not go to Gilgal; do not go up to Beth Aven...* (Hos. 4:15).

- *Is Gilead wicked? Its people are worthless! Do they sacrifice bulls in Gilgal? Their altars will be like piles of stones on a plowed field* (Hos. 12:11).

- *Go to Bethel and sin; go to Gilgal and sin yet more. Bring your sacrifices every morning, your tithes every three years"* (Amos 4:4). This was a place where true worship of God had degenerated into centers of false teaching and apostasy.

May the centers of today's prophetic activity remain strong in their commitment to the King of kings. May you receive power to stand for what is righteous.

Have you stood firm for moral, ethical, and spiritual standards when challenged?

A Time of Preparation

Then the LORD said to Abraham, "Why did Sarah laugh and say, 'Will I really have a child, now that I am old?' Is anything too hard for the LORD? I will return to you at the appointed time next year and Sarah will have a son" (Genesis 18:13-14).

A time of barrenness may be the time of preparation. God was preparing Sarah for motherhood. You too can make the best of whatever barren situation you encounter just as these people did in Bible days.

Rebekah. *"Isaac prayed to the LORD on behalf of his wife, because she was childless. The LORD answered his prayer, and his wife Rebekah became pregnant"* (Gen. 25:21).

Rachael. *"When the LORD saw that Leah was not loved, he enabled her to conceive, but Rachel remained childless. Leah became pregnant and gave birth to a son. ..."Now at last my husband will become attached to me, because I have borne him three sons." So he was named Levi. She conceived again, and when she gave birth to a son she said, "This time I will praise the LORD." So she named him Judah. Then she stopped having children* (Gen. 29:31-39).

May God use your wilderness experience to prepare you for His purpose in your life.

**Do you know for what purpose
God is preparing you?**

Cause to Rejoice

Then, led by Jehoshaphat, all the men of Judah and Jerusalem returned joyfully to Jerusalem, for the Lord had given them cause to rejoice over their enemies (2 Chronicles 20:27)

G OD will give you cause to rejoice over your enemies. You will be given power and wisdom to overcome your adversaries as you walk in His will for your life.

What causes you to rejoice?

The Benefits of Esther's Fast

"Go, gather together all the Jews that are present in Shushan, and fast for me; and neither eat nor drink for three days, night or day. I also and my maids will fast as you do. Then I will go to the king, though it is against the law; and if I perish, I perish." So Mordecai went away and did all that Esther had commanded him (Esther 4:15-17).

E STHER's fast leads to the presence of the king—a metaphor of the Lord our God. In His presence is relief, deliverance, help, and favor will come from the throne of God. Esther and her maids were an army of royal intercessors who boldly approached His throne in majestic robes on behalf of the people of God.

You can do the same. Pray for:

- The King to be pleased with you and hold out His gold scepter to you.

- Uncommon favor from the Lord.

- The blessings of Joseph—that the land will be blessed and for *"the precious dews from heaven, with deep waters that lies below, the best the sun brings forth, the finest the moon can yield, the choicest gifts of ancient mountains and the fruitfulness of the everlasting hills"* (Deut. 33:13-15).

What are your thoughts and beliefs about fasting?

The Benefits of Esther's Fast,
Continued

Yet having learned who Mordecai's people were, he scorned the idea of killing only Mordecai. Instead Haman looked for a way to destroy all Mordecai's people, the Jews, throughout the whole kingdom of Xerxes (Esther 3:6).

THIS is the fast that leads to the place of favor, that brings help from God, turns the table against the enemy of God's people, brings salvation to the city, and averts any seen and unseen calamity.

The benefits of Esther's fast include:

1. Honor and promotion instead of shame and reproach.

2. God will turn the tables against your enemy (see Esther 9:1).

3. Deliverance, glory, and faith.

4. The grace of God's second chance will be available to you.

5. His covenant of mercy, restoration, new beginning, fresh start, fruitfulness, increase, multiplication, and occupation (see Gen. 9:1-3).

Have you benefited from fasting?

Esther Defeats Evil

*When the perishable has been clothed with the imperishable,
and the mortal with immortality, then the saying that is written will come true: "Death has been swallowed up in victory"*
(1 Corinthians 15:54).

J UST as the prayers and fasting led by Esther brought the aversion
of the evil plans of Haman, so God will also frustrate all evil plans
against you. God will grant you victory on every side (see 1 Chron.
18:6).

*The king said, "Impale him on it!" So they impaled Haman
on the pole he had set up for Mordecai. Then the king's fury
subsided* (Esther 7:9-10).

**Do you believe that God
can turn defeat into victory?**

The God of Every Season

Those who hope in the Lord will renew their strength. They will soar on wings like eagles; they will run and not grow weary, they will walk and not be faint (Isaiah 40:31).

THE prophet Isaiah confirmed that God is the God of every season when he said that He will renew our strength. No matter what we are going through, no matter what has drained our strength and caused us to be less than 100 percent—if we hope in the Lord, He will refresh and revive us.

This is God's blessing and enablement for all seasons that will come across your path in life. Whether you are in the season of running or walking, God is able to help and deliver!

Are you feeling weary?
Have you put your hope in the Lord?

Stand Firm

*If you do not stand firm in your faith,
you will not stand at all* (Isaiah 7:9b).

Resist the spirit of frustration! Your victory is assured. Do not take notice of the devil whether he appears to be silent or active. Even when the enemy appears to be doing nothing, the least he is actually doing is trying to wear you out.

That is why the Bible says, *"the kindest acts of the wicked are cruel"* (Prov. 12:10)!

And always remember, *"Submit yourselves, then, to God. **Resist the devil**, and he will flee from you"* (James 4:7).

Are you standing firm and resisting the devil?

Never Give Up Your Dreams

M ANY memorable statements were accredited to the apostle Paul. Here are some to bless you:

Paul said, *"So keep up your courage, men, for I have faith in God that it will happen just as he told me"* (Acts 27:25). Never give up your dream; you will not fail!

You will not fail because *"the righteous will live by faith"* (Rom. 1:17). Keep hope alive!

With God nothing is impossible, Paul said, *"why should anyone consider it impossible that God can raise the dead"* (Acts 26:8). Speak life into any good thing that is dead around you.

After all, at the end of it all, you should say like Paul, *"So then...I was not disobedient to the vision from heaven"* (Acts 26:19). That is what counts!

**Can you accept and speak these blessings
as Paul did?**

Connecting with God's Economy

And the LORD will make a difference between the livestock of Israel and the livestock of Egypt. So nothing shall die of all that belongs to the children of Israel (Exodus 9:4 NKJV).

PRAY to be connected with the economy of God. This is the same principle as the Goshen economy—the blessings that were upon Goshen as written in Exodus 9:4.

Being connected to God's economy includes putting the following into practice:

1. Make note of what works to maximize the moment.
2. Recognize the season for opening your eyes to see into the spiritual realm; to see what God is doing.
3. To participate with what God is doing; be part of the army of God.
4. As we cross over to our Promised Land we lay the burden of this world at His feet.
5. Pray for women to be given their rightful places in the leadership of the church of God.

Pray on these things and the God of peace will guard your heart and mind in Christ Jesus.

Do you feel connected to God's economy?

Out of the Blazing Furnace

"Now when you hear the sound of the horn, flute, zither, lyre, harp, pipe and all kinds of music, if you are ready to fall down and worship the image I made, very good. But if you do not worship it, you will be thrown immediately into a blazing furnace. Then what god will be able to rescue you from my hand?" Shadrach, Meshach and Abednego replied to him, "King Nebuchadnezzar, we do not need to defend ourselves before you in this matter. **If we are thrown into the blazing furnace, the God we serve is able to deliver us from it, and he will deliver us from Your Majesty's hand. But even if he does not, we want you to know, Your Majesty, that we will not serve your gods or worship the image of gold you have set up"**
(Daniel 3:15-18).

TRULY, God showed up on their behalf, *"Look! I see four men walking around in the fire, unbound and unharmed, and the fourth looks like a son of the gods." Nebuchadnezzar then approached the opening of the blazing furnace and shouted, "Shadrach, Meshach and Abednego, servants of the Most High God, come out! Come here!" So Shadrach, Meshach and Abednego came out of the fire, and the satraps, prefects, governors and royal advisers crowded around them. They saw that the fire had not harmed their bodies, nor was a hair of their heads singed; their robes were not scorched, and there was no smell of fire on them"* (Dan. 3:25-27).

Put your trust in God, and you will never be disappointed.

How trusting are you of God's deliverance?

No God Like Jehovah

Even the wicked, erratic, and unpredictable King Nebuchadnezzar acknowledges that no other God can save like our God, *"Then Nebuchadnezzar said, "Praise be to the God of Shadrach, Meshach and Abednego, who has sent his angel and rescued his servants! They trusted in him and defied the king's command and were willing to give up their lives rather than serve or worship any god except their own God. Therefore I decree that the people of any nation or language who say anything against the God of Shadrach, Meshach and Abednego be cut into pieces and their houses be turned into piles of rubble, for no other god can save in this way"* (Dan. 3:28-29).

There is no God like Jehovah.

**Who was in the fiery furnace with
Shadrach, Meshach, and Abednego?**

The Revealer of Mysteries

*Daniel replied, "No wise man, enchanter, magician or diviner can explain to the king the mystery he has asked about, but there is a **God in heaven who reveals mysteries.** He has shown King Nebuchadnezzar what will happen in days to come. Your dream and the visions that passed through your mind as you were lying in bed are these: As Your Majesty was lying there, your mind turned to things to come, and **the revealer of mysteries** showed you what is going to happen. As for me, this mystery has been revealed to me, not because I have greater wisdom than anyone else alive, but so that Your Majesty may know the interpretation and that you may understand what went through your mind"* (Daniel 2:27-30).

Gᴏᴅ knows everything; nothing is hidden before Him, and He reveals His secret to those who fear Him. Daniel testifies that God is the Revealer of mysteries.

Today, ask Him to share His secret with you and be a step ahead of your enemies!

What mysteries do you want revealed by the Revealer?

Being Found

Arioch took Daniel to the king at once and said, "I have found a man among the exiles from Judah who can tell the king what his dream means" (Daniel 2:25).

D ANIEL was found and then was taken to the king. There he used his God-given gift to tell the king what his dream meant.

God gives each of His children a gift, or gifts. Develop your potentials and protect your gifting, someday you will be *found* by those who are in authority. Your time will come and the gift will make a way for you.

Are you developing your skills and increasing your knowledge?

Give Credit to Others

I [Daniel] *thank and praise you, God of my ancestors: You have given me wisdom and power, you have made known to me what we asked of you, you have made known to us the dream of the king. This was the dream, and now we will interpret it to the king* (Daniel 2:23,36).

IN actual sense, the mystery was revealed to Daniel; but he realized his friend's prayers made the difference! It was Daniel who actually gave the interpretation, but he said, *"we* will interpret it to the king."

No matter your giftedness, remember that others have made it possible for you to get to where you are.

How willing are you to give credit to others?

He Changes Times and Seasons

He changes times and seasons; he deposes kings and raises up others. He gives wisdom to the wise and knowledge to the discerning (Daniel 2:21).

A LL power belongs to God!

God decides the times and the seasons and He is the One who makes the only positive and significant difference in your life.

Your season is about to change for good.

Are you ready for some good to come into your life?

Reading the Bible in a Year: Isaiah 29-30 & Ephesians 6.

No Babylonian Language

Then the king ordered Ashpenaz, chief of his court officials, to bring into the king's service some of the Israelites from the royal family and the nobility—young men without any physical defect, handsome, showing aptitude for every kind of learning, well informed, quick to understand, and qualified to serve in the king's palace. He was to teach them the language and literature of the Babylonians. The king assigned them a daily amount of food and wine from the king's table. They were to be trained for three years, and after that they were to enter the king's service (Daniel 1:3-6).

IF you speak the Babylonian language, you create a Babylonian atmosphere around you, which is not good. This was the strategy of the king of Babylon in recruiting young and talented youths from Israel: feed them with Babylonian food (wrong doctrine), then pollute their minds and infiltrate their thinking systems. Out of their confused minds, their mouths will speak the Babylonian language, because out of the heart's overflow, the mouth speaks.

Your words frame the world around you!

How are your words affecting others?
Are they uplifting or discouraging?

Seeing into the Spirit Realm

Then King Nebuchadnezzar leaped to his feet in amazement and asked his advisers, "Weren't there three men that we tied up and threw into the fire?" They replied, "Certainly, Your Majesty." He said, "Look! I see four men walking around in the fire, unbound and unharmed, and the fourth looks like a son of the gods." Nebuchadnezzar then approached the opening of the blazing furnace and shouted, "Shadrach, Meshach and Abednego, servants of the Most High God, come out! Come here!" So Shadrach, Meshach and Abednego came out of the fire (Daniel 3:24-26).

IN his depraved state, even Nebuchadnezzar was still able to see into the spirit realm. Because that is true, how much more should believers see into the spirit realm? Have you prayed for this gift?

Have you seen into the spiritual realm?

His Mighty Wonders

How great are his signs, how mighty his wonders! His kingdom is an eternal kingdom; his dominion endures from generation to generation (Daniel 4:3).

DANIEL recognized that God is mighty, His signs are great, and that His Kingdom will endure for many generations. The faith he had in God brought him to a place where he could use his gift to bring about God's purpose.

When believers don't use their gifts, God must use other ways to accomplish His goals. May you always be willing to allow God to use you to increase His Kingdom and to move you closer toward fulfilling your God-given destiny.

Are you focusing on God's mighty wonders and great signs?

God Interprets Dreams

*Now we have not received the spirit [that belongs to] the world, but the [Holy] Spirit Who is from God, [given to us] that we might realize and comprehend and appreciate the gifts [of divine favour and blessing so freely and lavishly] bestowed on us by God. And we are setting these truths forth in words not taught by human wisdom but **taught by the [Holy] Spirit, combining and interpreting spiritual truths with spiritual language** [to those who possess the Holy Spirit]. But the natural, nonspiritual man does not accept or welcome or admit into his heart the gifts and teachings and revelations of the Spirit of God, for they are folly (meaningless nonsense) to him; and he is incapable of knowing them [of progressively recognizing, understanding, and becoming better acquainted with them] because they are spiritually discerned and esti- mated and appreciated* (1 Corinthians 2:12-14 AMP).

THE passage from First Corinthians is very enlightening. It is worth study and contemplation, as is Daniel 4:7-8 and Genesis 40:8).

**Is the Holy Spirit at work in your life
teaching and revealing?**

Resolve to Serve God

*But **Daniel resolved not to defile himself** with the royal food and wine, and he asked the chief official for permission not to defile himself this way. Now God had caused the official to show favor and compassion to Daniel. At the end of the ten days they looked healthier and better nourished than any of the young men who ate the royal food. In every matter of wisdom and understanding about which the king questioned them, he found them ten times better than all the magicians and enchanters in his whole kingdom"* (Daniel 1:8-9,15,20).

E VERY day in every way you must resolve to serve God, otherwise the enemy is ready and waiting to slip into your life and defile it. When you choose to serve God, He will make you healthier, better nourished, wise, and with more understanding than all others.

Are you defiling yourself in subtle ways?

The Reward of Diligence

*To these four young men **God gave knowledge and understanding** of all kinds of literature and learning. And Daniel could understand visions and dreams of all kinds* (Daniel 1:17).

WHEN you commit to developing and improving your skills and talents, God will be faithful to give you knowledge and understanding in many areas, especially those that will enhance His Kingdom and your destiny.

Are you committed to improving your lot in life?

God's Tree

These are the visions I saw while lying in bed: I looked, and there before me stood a tree in the middle of the land. Its height was enormous. The tree grew large and strong and its top touched the sky; it was visible to the ends of the earth. Its leaves were beautiful, its fruit abundant, and on it was food for all. Under it the wild animals found shelter, and the birds lived in its branches; from it every creature was fed (Daniel 4:10-12).

I find this vision most interesting and believe that the tree symbolizes the following that we can take comfort in:

- The location was chosen by God.
- Fame and honor = "height was erroneous"
- Supernatural = "It grew large and strong"
- Renounced = "Visible to the ends of the earth"
- Its leaves = "Beautiful"
- Its fruits = "abundant"
- Food = "For All"
- Under it shelter = "the beasts of the field"
- In its branches = "the birds of the air lived"
- Every creature = "was fed"

**Has God planted a tree in your heart
that will bring Him glory?**

Humbling the Prideful

At the same time that my sanity was restored, my honor and splendour were returned to me for the glory of my kingdom. My advisers and nobles sought me out, and I was restored to my throne and became even greater than before. Now I, Nebuchadnezzar, praise and exalt and glorify the King of heaven, because **everything he [God] does is right and all his ways are just. And those who walk in pride he is able to humble** (Daniel 4:36-37).

BEING humbled is not an enjoyable experience. Nevertheless, it is essential for you to avoid a prideful life, which leads only to destruction.

But after Uzziah became powerful, his **pride** *led to his downfall. He was unfaithful to the LORD his God, and entered the temple of the LORD to burn incense on the altar of incense* (2 Chronicles 26:16).

For everything in the world—the lust of the flesh, the lust of the eyes, and the **pride** *of life—comes not from the Father but from the world* (1 John 2:16).

Has God had to humble you lately?

Learning from Mistakes

*So they brought in the gold goblets that had been taken from the temple of God in Jerusalem, and the king and his nobles, his wives and his concubines drank from them. As they drank the wine, they praised the gods of gold and silver, of bronze, iron, wood and stone. But when **his heart became arrogant and hardened with pride,** he was deposed from his royal throne and stripped of his glory. He was driven away from people and given the mind of an animal; he lived with the wild donkeys and ate grass like the ox; and his body was drenched with the dew of heaven, **until he acknowledged that the Most High God is sovereign** over all kingdoms on earth and sets over them anyone he wishes. "But you, Belshazzar, his son, have not humbled yourself, though you knew all this* (Daniel 5:3-4,20-22)

TERRIBLE things happen when your soul is prideful. Arrogance can turn you into someone that God and others don't want to be around. When you know someone whose life has been destroyed by pride and arrogance, learn from that person, don't make the same mistakes.

Have you learned from other's mistakes?

Reputation

"He did this because Daniel, whom the king called Belt-
eshazzar, was found to have a keen mind and knowledge
and understanding, and also the ability to interpret dreams,
explain riddles and solve difficult problems. Call for Dan-
iel, and he will tell you what the writing means." So Daniel
was brought before the king, and the king said to him, "Are
you Daniel, one of the exiles my father the king brought from
*Judah? **I have heard that the spirit of the gods is in you***
and that you have insight, intelligence and outstanding
wisdom" (Daniel 5:12-14).

D ANIEL'S reputation was that he had insight, intelligence, and
outstanding wisdom. I have no doubt that he worked hard to
maintain that reputation and that God rewarded him for it.

I pray that your reputation is an accurate reflection of you, and
that you will work hard to maintain it for His glory.

What have others heard about you?

Hidden Meaning

*"This is the inscription that was **written**: MENE, MENE, TEKEL, PARSIN Here is what these words **mean**: Mene: God has numbered the days of your reign and brought it to an end. Tekel: You have been weighed on the scales and found wanting. Peres: Your kingdom is divided and given to the Medes and Persians"* (Daniel 5:25-28).

As mentioned previously, you need God or one of His servants to interpret the meaning of dreams, inscriptions, and other spiritual messages, because our finite minds cannot understand without His help.

Is there something for which you need help interpreting the meaning?

No Corruption in Him

At this, the administrators and the satraps tried to find grounds for charges against Daniel in his conduct of government affairs, but they were unable to do so. They could find no corruption in him, because he was trustworthy and neither corrupt nor negligent (Daniel 6:4).

DANIEL was found to be *"trustworthy, and neither corrupt nor negligent."* It is so easy these days to take the easy way out, to cut corners, and to cheat just a little here and there. May you always be the same credible person when you are alone as you are when others are nearby.

If someone was investigating, would you be found trustworthy and incorruptible?

Turning to God

Now when Daniel learned that the decree had been pub-
lished, he went home to his upstairs room where the win-
dows opened toward Jerusalem. ***Three times a day he***
got down on his knees and prayed, giving thanks to his
God, *just as he had done before. Then these men went as a*
group and found Daniel praying and asking God for help
(Daniel 6:10-11).

I N times of trouble who do you turn to on the day that is evil, do you
seek out friends, clergy, your horoscope? Daniel sought God three
times a day in prayer and thanksgiving. Jesus said to Peter, *"Simon,*
Simon, Satan has asked to sift you as wheat. but I have prayed for
you that your faith may not fail" (Luke 22:31-32). This is what matters! *"If you do not stand firm in your faith, you will not stand at all"*
(Isa. 7:9b). Daniel held on to God! May you always follow his good
example and turn to God when troubles come your way.

Are you turning to God when faced with turmoil
or grievous circumstances?

The Distinction

*The king was overjoyed and gave orders to lift Daniel out of the den. And when Daniel was lifted from the den, no wound was found on him, **because he had trusted in his God.** At the king's command, the men who had falsely accused Daniel were brought in and thrown into the lions' den, along with their wives and children. And before they reached the floor of the den, the lions overpowered them and crushed all their bones* (Daniel 6:23-24).

*And you will again see **the distinction between the righteous and the wicked,** between those who serve God and those who do not* (Malachi 3:18).

THERE is a distinction between the righteous and the wicked—between those who trust in God and serve Him and those who don't. This passage from Daniel 6 is a terrible reminder of what happens to those who falsely accuse.

Can you be counted among those who are righteous, trusting, and serving God?

Jesus—the Door

I [Jesus] am the gate; whoever enters through me will be saved. They will come in and go out, and find pasture. The thief comes only to steal and kill and destroy; I have come that they may have life, and have it to the full (John 10:9-10).

JESUS as the Door is a metaphor of divine opening. When you recognize Jesus as the Door that opens to a pasture of unlimited resources, you will see Him face to face.

A great Door, good and effectual, is opened to you, *"After I go through Macedonia, I will come to you—for I will be going through Macedonia. Perhaps I will stay with you for a while, or even spend the winter, so that you can help me on my journey, wherever I go. For I do not want to see you now and make only a passing visit; I hope to spend some time with you, if the Lord permits. But I will stay on at Ephesus until Pentecost, because* **a great door for effective work** *has opened to me, and there are many who oppose me"* (1 Cor. 16:5-9).

There will be divine removal of limitation, *"This is what the LORD says to his anointed, to Cyrus, whose right hand I take hold of to subdue nations before him and to strip kings of their armor, to* **open doors** *before him so that gates will not be shut"* (Isaiah 45:1).

Are you ready to walk through the open doors that lead to Jesus and His anointing?

The Zeal of the Lord

*For to us a child is born, to us a son is given, and the government will be on his shoulders. And he will be called Wonderful Counsellor, Mighty God, Everlasting Father, Prince of Peace. Of the greatness of his government and peace there will be no end. He will reign on David's throne and over his kingdom, establishing and upholding it with justice and righteousness from that time on and forever. **The zeal of the LORD Almighty will accomplish this** (Isaiah 9:6-7).*

A FTER the Bible declares all the great names and attributes of Jesus Christ, then we are told how it would be accomplished—"the zeal of the Lord will accomplish it." Jesus' disciples saw the passion with which He drove away the traders and robbers from the temple and instantly remembered it is written that the "zeal of the house of God" will consume Him.

Let the zeal of the Lord propel you to your accomplishment!

The next several days depict examples of people with the zeal of God in the Bible.

What comes to mind when you hear or read the word zeal?

The Zeal of the Lord,
Continued

*N*ow King David was told, "The LORD has blessed the household of Obed-Edom and everything he has, because of the ark of God." So David went to bring up the ark of God from the house of Obed-Edom to the City of David with rejoicing. When those who were carrying the ark of the LORD had taken six steps, he sacrificed a bull and a fattened calf. Wearing a linen ephod, David was dancing before the LORD with all his might, while he and all Israel were bringing up the ark of the LORD with shouts and the sound of trumpets" (2 Sam. 6:12-15). The zeal of King David was for the things of God—the tabernacle of praise.

When all the elders of Israel had arrived, the priests took up the ark, and they brought up the ark of the LORD and the tent of meeting and all the sacred furnishings in it. The priests and Levites carried them up, and King Solomon and the entire assembly of Israel that had gathered about him were before the ark, sacrificing so many sheep and cattle that they could not be recorded or counted." Then Solomon said, "The LORD has said that he would dwell in a dark cloud; I have indeed built a magnificent temple for you, a place for you to dwell forever" (1 Kings 8:3-5,12-13). The zeal of King Solomon was for the ark—every six steps, his entourage praised and sacrificed to God.

How zealous are you for the things of God and to praise and sacrifice for Him?

The Zeal of the Lord,
Continued

*N*ow there was a man in Jerusalem called Simeon, who was righteous and devout. He was waiting for the consolation of Israel, and the Holy Spirit was on him. It had been revealed to him by the Holy Spirit that he would not die before he had seen the Lord's Messiah. Moved by the Spirit, he went into the temple courts. When the parents brought in the child Jesus to do for him what the custom of the Law required, Simeon took him in his arms and praised God* (Luke 2:25-28). Simeon's zeal was waiting for the consolation of Israel.

There was also a prophet, Anna, the daughter of Penuel, of the tribe of Asher. She was very old; she had lived with her husband seven years after her marriage, and then was a widow until she was eighty-four. She never left the temple but worshiped night and day, fasting and praying. Coming up to them at that very moment, she gave thanks to God and spoke about the child to all who were looking forward to the redemption of Jerusalem (Luke 2:36-38). Prophetess Anna was married for seven years and a widow for 77 years, she zealously devoted her life to praying for the coming Messiah.

**How easy would it be for you to wait as
Simeon and Anna did?**

The Zeal of the Lord,
Continued

When Jonah's warning reached the king of Nineveh, he rose from his throne...issued..."By the decree of the king and his nobles: Do not let people or animals, herds or flocks, taste anything; do not let them eat or drink. But let people and animals be covered with sackcloth. Let everyone call urgently on God. Let them give up their evil ways and their violence. ... When God saw what they did and how they turned from their evil ways, he relented and did not bring on them the destruction he had threatened (Jon. 3:6-10).

THE king of Nineveh heard the warning from God and declared a national fast for men and animals; his zeal included the extraordinary step of fasting of livestock.

And there was a man called Zacchaeus...climbed up in a sycamore tree in order to see Him...when Jesus reached the place, He looked up and said to him, Zacchaeus, hurry and come down; for I must stay at your house today. ...So then Zacchaeus stood up and solemnly declared to the Lord, See, Lord, the half of my goods I [now] give [by way of restoration] to the poor, and if I have cheated anyone out of anything, I [now] restore four times as much. And Jesus said to him, Today is Messianic and spiritual] salvation come to [all the members of] this household, since Zacchaeus too is a [real spiritual] son of Abraham; For the Son of Man came to seek and to save that which was lost" (Luke 19:10 AMP).

The zeal of Zacchaeus, the tax collector, made him climb a tree, ready to give away half of his riches, and to restore four times what he cheated out of people.

What does zealousness for Jesus make you do?

Abundant Peace and Security

*"...I will bring you together again like sheep in a pen like a flock in its pasture. Yes, your land will again be filled **with noisy, happy crowds**!"* (Micah 2:12 Living Bible)

A happy crowd once again Micah writes about. Health, healing, abundant peace and security for them—and for you and all your loved ones, I pray.

"I will bring health and healing to it; I will heal my people and will let them enjoy abundant peace and security" (Jeremiah 33:6).

There will be double destruction for the enemies of God's plans, *"Let my persecutors be put to shame, but keep me from shame; let them be terrified, but keep me from terror. Bring on them the day of disaster; destroy them with double destruction"* (Jer. 17:18).

What does abundant peace and security mean to you?

The Time of God's Favor

As God's co-workers we urge you not to receive God's grace in vain. For he says, "In the time of my favor I heard you, and in the day of salvation I helped you." I tell you, **now is the time of God's favor,** *now is the day of salvation* (2 Corinthians 6:1).

- Pray that God will bring all contentious issues to the valley of Jehoshaphat, the place where God judges (see Joel 3:2) and give you victory.
- Pray that God will strengthen you, save you from all troubles, and restore you (see Zech. 10:6).
- Pray that God will leave a blessing instead of a curse (see Joel 2:14; Jonah 3:6-10).
- Pray that your help will come from God (2 Kings 6:27; Ps. 121).
- Pray that you will show the evidence of His discipleship—the power of God in your life (see Acts 1:8; Mal. 3:18; Exod. 33:15-16).
- Pray that none of His good promises concerning you will fail (Josh. 23:14b).

Living in God's favor is the most perfect place to be. May these prayers bring you into His favor and keep you there until you meet Him face to face.

Have you received God's grace in vain?

The "Even Now Miracle"

"Lord," Martha said to Jesus, "if you had been here, my brother would not have died. But I know that even now God will give you whatever you ask." Jesus said to her, "Your brother will rise again" (John 11:21-23).

COME to Him with expectation and a repentant heart; He will not despise a contrite heart. Martha gave up all hope, but somehow she was prompted to remember that there was an "even now God" who could "give you whatever you ask."

I wish you an "even now miracle" from a God who can turn things around for your good "even if things" don't look that great!

As the Lord declares, *"Even now...return to me with all your heart, with fasting and weeping and mourning"* (Hos. 2:12).

Your "Lazarus" will rise again.

Even now do you approach God with expectation and a repentant heart?

God's *Rhema* Word

When He had finished speaking, He said to Simon; "Now go out where it is deeper and let down your nets and you will catch a lot of fish" (Luke 5:4 Living Bible).

I N a way, the Bible is the Word of God speaking generally to every-body. But what He says to you on a personal level is your personal, God *rhema* word to you! Like Peter, the key to your big catch (your breakthrough) is in your personal word from God.

Listen to His personal word to your spirit, because it activates, stirs up, and brings birthing to your spirit!

You are a word away from a breakthrough in your life!

Are you listening for your *rhema* word from God?

Valley Experiences

*There I will give her back her vineyards, and will make the
Valley of Achor* [Trouble] *a door of hope* (Hosea 2:14-15).

Pray that God will turn your valley experiences around for your good, and that:

- Any Valley of Achor will become a door of hope.

- Every valley of Baca will become a place of fresh springs, *"Passing through the Valley of Weeping* [Baca], *they make it a place of springs; the early rain also fills* [the pools] *with blessings"* (Ps. 84:6).

- Every daunting challenge will become a place of blessing (Beracah) (see 2 Chron. 20 24-26).

- God will bring your enemies to the Valley of Jehoshaphat (where God judges) and grant you justice (see Joel 3:1,12).

- God gives you divine momentum to avenge your enemies as in the Valley of Ajalon; (see Josh. 10:12).

- In the Valley of Elah, the battle becomes the war of gods (see 1 Sam. 17:19-49).

**How can you help God to turn your valley
experiences into doorways of hope?**

You Will Abound

*And God is able to make all grace abound to you, so that in all things at all times, having all you need, **you will abound in every good work** (2 Corinthians 9:8).*

G OD's grace is in you, you will have all things at all times and you will abound in good works.

*All Scripture is God-breathed and is useful for teaching, rebuking, correcting and training in righteousness, so that the servant of God may be thoroughly equipped **for every good work** (2 Timothy 3:16-17).*

Although you are not saved by works, good works do play an important role in your life as a believer. Jesus went about doing good works for those in need. You, too, are encouraged to help your neighbor, or co-worker, all those who are hurting, suffering, and need your help.

What does it mean to you to "abound in every good work"?

Heart Intentions

*"Who touched me?" ...Peter said, "Master, so many are crowding against you...." But Jesus replied "no, it was someone who **deliberately** touched me for, I felt healing power go out from me"* (Luke 8:45-46 Living Bible).

THIS is the popular story of the woman with the issue of blood, and Jesus' emphasis was on what she purposed in her heart. Far away from where Jesus was, she had truly purposed in her heart, *"For she said to herself, "If only I may touch His garment, I shall be made well."*

She received her miracle that day. What eluded her for 12 years, she got in an instant. The key to divine power is connected to the intentions of our heart rather than the mere exterior of our actions! People look at your outside, but God looks inside. The interior of our being is of paramount importance, and that is why the Bible says as a person thinks, so is he.

Don't just join the crowd, be transformed by the renewal of your heart (see 2 Cor. 4:16).

In what condition is your heart?

Your First Kingdom Duty

But the man from whom the demons had gone out kept begging and praying that he might accompany Him and be with Him, but [Jesus] sent him away, saying, **Return to your home, and recount [the story] of how many and great things God has done for you.** *And [the man] departed, proclaiming throughout the whole city how much Jesus had done for him* (Luke 8:38-39 AMP).

WHEN Jesus healed the demon-possessed man of Gadarene, Jesus told him what his first assignment in the Kingdom was, *"Return to your home, and recount [the story] of how many and great things God has done for you."*

The same is true for our assignment; and indeed, what is the first ministry of every born-again believer? Your first duty in the Kingdom is to give your testimony beginning with your family and household.

Have you recently given your testimony?

Breaking the Vow of Poverty

For you know the grace of our Lord Jesus Christ, that though he was rich, yet for your sake he became poor, so that you through his poverty might become rich (2 Corinthians 8:9).

PRAY to break any generational vows of poverty, *"His father Isaac answered him, "Your dwelling will be away from the earth's richness, away from the dew of heaven above. …But when you grow restless, you will throw his yoke from off your neck"* (Gen. 27:39-40).

Esau eventually broke the curse for Esau became rich, *"Esau asked, 'What is the meaning of all these flocks and herds I met?' 'To find favor in your eyes, my lord,' he said. But Esau said, 'I already have plenty, my brother. Keep what you have for yourself'"* (Gen. 33:8-9).

May you and generations after you be prosperous and generous. May you always have enough and enough to share with others.

**Have you thrown the yoke of poverty from
your neck and reaped His bounty?**

Pursue! Overtake! Recover All!

*Pursue, for you shall surely **overtake** them and without fail **recover all*** (1 Samuel 30:8).

Pursue. *"When Abram heard that his relative had been taken captive, he called out the 318 trained men born in his household and went in **pursuit** as far as Dan"* (Gen. 14:14).

Overtake. *"The days are coming," declares the LORD, "when the reaper will be **overtaken** by the ploughman and the planter by the one treading grapes. New wine will drip from the mountains and flow from all the hills"* (Amos 9:13). *"And all these blessings shall come upon you and **overtake** you, because you obey the voice of the LORD your God"* (Deut. 28:2). Evidently, the earth's riches were no longer far from his dwelling.

Recover all—restore. *"So I will **restore** to you the years that the swarming locust has eaten, the crawling locust, the consuming locust, and the chewing locust, My great army which I sent among you"* (Joel 2:25 NKJV).

> Do you agree that it is time for you to pursue, overtake, and recover all that you have lost?

Signs of the Times

*And of Issachar, men who had **understanding of the times** to know what Israel ought to do, 200 chiefs; and all their kinsmen were under their command* (1 Chronicles 12:32).

D o not be troubled when you see or hear of the signs of the times. They are the beginning of wealth transfer to the Kingdom of God! It was said of the sons of Issachar that they understood the times.

You, too, will have understanding of the times when you trust in the Lord with all your heart and listen closely for His voice telling you what you ought to do.

What signs of the times have you witnessed lately?

Protected by the Word

...the people were trying to kill him [Jesus Christ]. *Yet they could not find any way to do it, because all the people hung on his words* (Luke 19:47-48).

I N His humanity, Jesus was protected by the Word of God. The people tried to kill Him but they forgot one thing—*"all the people hung on His words."* Truly, He sustains all things by the power of the word (Heb. 1:3)

As you leave home today, take the Word with you! God upholds everything by the word of His power (see Heb. 1:3).

Have you made the Word of God your shield?

Keep Praying

One day Jesus told His disciples a story to illustrate their need for constant prayer and to show them that they must keep praying until the answer comes (Luke 18:1 Living Bible).

W E must keep on praying until the Lord answers our prayers. This is what Luke recorded that Jesus told His disciples. He also told them another story and concluded, *"For the proud shall be humbled but the humble shall be honored"* (Luke 18:14b Living Bible).

You are blessed and highly favored—keep praying until your answer comes. God is faithful to answer your prayers, be alert to answers that may be unexpected.

Is prayer part of your everyday routine?

Fear the Lord

As for me, far be it from me that I should sin against the LORD by failing to pray for you. And I will teach you the way that is good and right. **But be sure to fear the LORD and serve him faithfully with all your heart;** *consider what great things he has done for you. Yet if you persist in doing evil, both you and your king will be swept away* (1 Samuel 12:23-24).

FEARING the Lord is not an option, throughout the Bible believers are told to fear Him.

*The **fear** of the LORD is the beginning of **wisdom**; all who follow his precepts have good understanding. To him belongs eternal praise* (Psalm 111:10).

*The **fear** of the LORD is the beginning of **wisdom**, and knowledge of the Holy One is understanding* (Proverbs 9:10).

*He will be the sure foundation for your times, a rich store of salvation and **wisdom** and knowledge; the **fear** of the LORD is the key to this treasure* (Isaiah 33:6).

Do you have a healthy fear and respect for the Lord your God?

Filled with the Spirit

*For he shall be great in the sight of the Lord, and shall drink neither wine nor strong drink; and he [John the Baptist] **shall be filled with the Holy Ghost,** even from his mother's womb* (Luke 1:15).

THOUGH John the Baptist lived before Jesus Christ was born on earth, he was filled with Holy Spirit from his mother's womb. What a privilege! He was almost like the present-day believer! His connection and relationship with Jesus Christ and being filled with Holy Spirit made him greater than any other Old Testament personalities.

Our time has come and God has given us reason to rejoice! The best is yet to come!

I believe that the unprecedented manifestation of the power of God has come.

Have you been filled with the Spirit?

The Promise of Increase

The farmer sows the word. Others, like seed sown on good soil, hear the word, accept it, and produce a crop—some thirty, some sixty, some a hundred times what was sown (Mark 4:14,20).

I pray that the promise of 30, 60, and 100 fold increase has begun in your life with new opportunities such as:

1. The tree of life will be restored to you, *"Then the angel showed me the river of the water of life, as clear as crystal, flowing from the throne of God and of the Lamb.... On each side of the river stood the tree of life, bearing twelve crops of fruit, yielding its fruit every month. And the leaves of the tree are for the healing of the nations. No longer will there be any curse..."* (Rev. 22:1-3).

2. Doors will be opened to you that no one can shut, *"After this I looked, and there before me was a door standing open in heaven. And the voice...said, "Come up here, and I will show you what must take place after this." At once I was in the Spirit..."* (Rev. 4:1-3).

In what areas of your life would you like increase?

God's Way Is Perfect

*As for God, **his way is perfect:** the LORD's word is flawless;*
he shields all who take refuge in him (2 Samuel 22:31).

God's way is perfect, and throughout the Bible He gives you ways to determine His way. I pray the following for you today:

That the Lord will be your Deliverer, *"The LORD is my rock, my fortress and my deliverer; my God is my rock, in whom I take refuge, my shield and the horn of my salvation, my stronghold* (Ps. 18:2).

That you will be delivered and gain possessions, *"But upon mount Zion shall be deliverance, and there shall be holiness; and the house of Jacob shall possess their possessions"* (Obadiah 1:17 KJV).

That God will remember you, *"Early the next morning they arose and worshiped before the LORD...and the LORD remembered her"* (1 Sam. 1:19).

How has God proven to you that His way is perfect?

Your Appointed Time Has Come

There is a time for everything, and a season for every activity under the heavens (Ecclesiastes 3:1).

IT is time for God to act and cut off anything that hinders you from attaining your destiny, *"It is time for You to act, O LORD, For they have regarded Your law as void"* (Ps. 119:126 NKJV).

Your time for uncommon favor, unprecedented and unparalleled, has come you, *"You will arise and have mercy on Zion; for the time to favor her, Yes, the set time, has come"* (Ps. 102:13 NKJV).

Your time for manifestation has come, *"So the child grew and became strong in spirit, and was in the deserts till the day of his manifestation to Israel"* (Luke 1:80 NKJV).

Your time for power is now, *"The LORD shall send the rod of thy strength out of Zion: rule thou in the midst of thine enemies. Thy people shall be willing in the day of thy power, in the beauties of holiness from the womb of the morning: thou hast the dew of thy youth"* (Ps. 110:2-3).

Are you ready to grasp your time of appointment?

Power to Belong to God

For the kingdom of God is not a matter of talk but of power
(1 Corinthians 4:20).

God has spoken plainly, and I have heard it many times:
Power, O God, belongs to you (Psalm 62:11-12 NLT).

L ET His Kingdom and power reign in your life beginning today.

How has the power of God been
manifested in your life?

The Lord Needs You

"Untie him" Jesus said, "And bring him here. And if anyone
asks you what you are doing, just say, "The Lord needs him"
(Luke 19:30b-31 Living Bible).

I heard this in my spirit one morning: The great destiny in you shall not be tied any longer! Why? The Lord has need of it. May God's purposes in your life be fulfilled. May every limitation in your life be broken by the power of His Word concerning you.

This is your moment! This is your time!

The Lord has come your way and every hold of limitation is now broken! This is freedom to move into your destiny.

**Can you feel the ropes untied and
hear the freedom He speaks?**

For Zion's Sake

For Zion's sake I will not hold My peace, and for Jerusalem's sake I will not rest, until her righteousness goes forth as brightness, and her salvation as a lamp that burns. I have set watchmen on your walls, O Jerusalem; they shall never hold their peace day or night. You who make mention of the LORD, do not keep silent, and give Him no rest till He establishes and till He makes Jerusalem a praise in the earth (Isaiah 62:1,6-7 NKJV).

THE purpose why we do a thing is important to God. So then let our purpose always be in line with His purpose. Here the Bible says for Zion's sake you should be persistent in calling upon the Lord until He establishes Jerusalem as a praise on earth. This is one of our reasonable services on the earth.

Can you be persistent enough until others see His righteousness and seek salvation?

Every Firstborn Male

Every male who opens the womb shall be called holy to the Lord (Luke 2:23 NKJV).

The LORD also said to Moses, "I have taken the Levites from among the Israelites in place of the first male offspring of every Israelite woman. The Levites are mine, for all the firstborn are mine. When I struck down all the firstborn in Egypt, I set apart for myself every firstborn in Israel, whether man or animal. They are to be mine. I am the LORD" (Numbers 3:11-13).

In the Old Testament, God asked for every male child who was a firstborn of any woman to be set apart for Him. In the New Testament, this was applied to Jesus Christ who was the male firstborn of Mary. Therefore, Jesus was both dedicated as required on the eighth day and sanctified as required above. I believe all first male children should continue to be especially sanctified to the service of God. Perhaps many have lost the benefits of this great ordinance!

Do you believe in the New Testament, all Old Testament requirements have been cancelled?

Hold on to Your Prophetic Message

*Here's a word you can take to heart and depend on: Jesus Christ came into the world to save sinners. I'm proof—Public Sinner Number One—of someone who could never have made it apart from sheer mercy. And now he shows me off—evidence of his endless patience—to those who are right on the edge of trusting him forever. ...I'm passing this work on to you, my son Timothy. The prophetic word that was **directed to you prepared us** for this. **All those prayers are coming together** now so you will do this well, fearless in your struggle, keeping a firm grip on your faith and on yourself. After all, **this is a fight we're in**. There are some, you know, who **by relaxing their grip and thinking anything goes have made a thorough mess** of their faith...* (1 Timothy 1:15-20 Message Bible).*

In this passage, Apostle Paul gives some of the benefits of the prophetic word:

1. *directed to you prepared us for* – for the future.
2. *All those prayers are coming together* – pray your prophetic word in the reality of your life.
3. *so you will do this well* – results in proper alignment with the will of God for your life.
4. *fearless in your struggle, keeping a firm grip on your faith and on yourself* – building up your faith and trust in God.
5. *this is a fight we're in* – we are in the battle for life.
6. *by relaxing their grip and thinking anything goes have made a thorough mess* – do not make a mess of your faith.

Do you have a prophetic word that needs to be realized in your life?

Family Ties

Has not the one God made you? You belong to him in body and spirit. And what does the one God seek? Godly offspring. So be on your guard, and do not be unfaithful to the wife of your youth (Malachi 2:15).

*But if a widow has children or grandchildren, these should learn first of all to put their religion into practice by caring for their own **family** and so repaying their parents and grand-parents, for this is pleasing to God* (1 Timothy 5:4).

*Resist him, standing firm in the faith, because you know that the **family** of believers throughout the world is undergoing the same kind of sufferings* (1 Peter 5:9).

As a member of the family of God and of your earthly family, I pray that you will care for them as you stand firm in the faith. Family members are meant to stick together and support each other. May this be your lot in life.

**How close are you to your relatives—
spiritual and earthly?**

The Race Is Not...

The race is not to the swift, nor the battle to the strong, nor bread to the wise, nor riches to men of understanding, nor favor to men of skill; but time and chance happen to them all (Ecclesiastes 9:11 NKJV).

I T is the Lord our God who counts!

Even though you may be a strong runner, strong in battles, and have the resources to buy off the judges of the race, you may not win just because time and chance happens to all, or as the Amplified Bible puts it, "sooner or later bad luck hits us all." It is who you put your trust in that really counts.

How does that "bad luck" statement fit in with your belief that God is in control?

Leave a Legacy

But Omri's followers proved stronger than those of Tibni son of Ginath. So Tibni died and Omri became king. In the thirty-first year of Asa king of Judah, Omri became king of Israel, and he reigned twelve years, six of them in Tirzah. He bought the hill of Samaria from Shemer for two talents of silver and built a city on the hill, calling it Samaria, after Shemer, the name of the former owner of the hill (1 Kings 16:22-24).

ALTHOUGH not many write or preach about Omri, he reigned for 12 years and his reign was impressive in terms of his accomplishments:

- Eliminated the initial opposition of Tibni.
- Captured more territories from Moab.
- Stopped the advancing Assyrian power.
- Built the new capital, Samaria.
- Assyria regarded Israel as the house of Omri.
- Omri was succeeded by Ahab his son.

God loves you so much that He has planned a living legacy for you to live. His plan includes eliminating opposition, gaining more resources, stopping the enemy, building His Kingdom, and not following the ways of the world or fleshly desires.

Are you living His legacy for you and are you leaving one for your children?

The Power of Unity

When they heard this, they raised their voices together in prayer to God... (Acts 4:24).

THERE are many instances in the Bible displaying the power of unity. Unity has power that should be put into godly use. One of these godly uses such as recorded in Second Chronicles 5:13, *"The trumpeters and musicians joined in unison to give praise and thanks to the LORD. Accompanied by trumpets, cymbals and other instruments, the singers raised their voices in praise to the LORD and sang: 'He is good; his love endures forever.'"* The result—temple was filled with God's palpable glory!

When the people raised their voices together in prayer to God in Acts 4:24, the result—*"the place where they were meeting was shaken. And they were all filled with the Holy Spirit and spoke the word of God boldly"* (Acts 4:31).

Today, I have an idea—why don't you bring people together in unity and raise your voices in praises and in prayers! There is no telling what He can do.

**Are you willing to gather people together
to praise and pray?**

The Power of Unity,
Continued

Now the whole earth had one language and one speech. And it came to pass, as they journeyed from the east, that they found a plain in the land of Shinar, and they dwelt there. Then they said to one another, "Come, let us make bricks and bake them thoroughly." They had brick for stone, and they had asphalt for mortar. And they said, "Come, let us build ourselves a city, and a tower whose top is in the heavens; let us make a name for ourselves, lest we be scattered abroad over the face of the whole earth." But the LORD came down to see the city and the tower which the sons of men had built. And the LORD said, "Indeed the people are one and they all have one language, and this is what they begin to do; now nothing that they propose to do will be withheld from them. Come, let Us go down and there confuse their language, that they may not understand one another's speech." So the LORD scattered them abroad from there over the face of all the earth, and they ceased building the city. Therefore its name is called Babel, because there the LORD confused the language of all the earth; and from there the LORD scattered them abroad over the face of all the earth (Genesis 11:1-10 NKJV).

SOMETIMES, people put the power of unity into wrong and ungodly purposes. I pray that God will grant you the wisdom to put the power of unity to godly use.

Have you witnessed a group of people who used their unity unrighteously?

Blessings

"Yes indeed, it won't be long now." God's Decree. "Things are going to happen so fast your head will swim; one thing fast on the heels of the other. You won't be able to keep up. Everything will be happening at once—and everywhere you look blessings! Blessings like wine pouring off the mountains and hills. I'll make everything right again for my people Israel: They'll rebuild their ruined cities. They'll plant vineyards and drink good wine. They'll work their gardens and eat fresh vegetables. And I'll plant them; plant them on their own land. They'll never again be uprooted from the land I've given them."
God, your God, says so" (Amos 9:13-15 Message Bible).

THIS God's decree is hard for me to take in—maybe because it will happen so fast that my "head will swim." There will be blessings "everywhere," and I, for one, am excited about this time. This is when God will make everything right for His people.

You will be eating and drinking goodness from the fields and gardens and you will never be pushed out of the way again. God's decree of blessing is for you to receive and enjoy.

Have you received your blessings today?

Walking with the Lord

He replied, The LORD, before whom I have walked faithfully, will send his angel with you and make your journey a success (Genesis 24:40).

PRAY as you walk with the Lord! Sometimes we fail because we should rest in His power; we wage war instead of relying on His supremacy over all situations. The following are some benefits of walking with God:

- Bonds of wickedness and chains of injustice would be loosed (see Isa. 58.6).
- Cords of heavy work would be untied.
- Oppressed would be set free.
- Every unrighteous yoke would be broken.
- No deceit would slip into your spirit (see Ps. 32:1-2).
- Hindrances to gaining understanding would be removed (see Ps. 32:5-9).

May you walk with the Lord in peace and love. May His mercy enfold you with every step you take together.

**How far are you prepared to walk
with your heavenly Father?**

Prayers of Sanctification

And Joshua said to the people, "Sanctify yourselves, for tomorrow the LORD will do wonders among you" (Joshua 3:5 NKJV).

THE need to call a holy fast and declare a period of sanctification should always be a priority as long as humankind lives in their earthen vessels.

For sanctification prayers, I suggest you use the following thoughts and Scripture:

- Psalm 119:133 (NKJV), *"let no iniquity have dominion over me."*

- You are washed by the blood of Jesus.

- Joshua 3:5 (NKJV), *"sanctify yourselves for tomorrow the Lord will do wonders among you"*

- 2 Chronicles 29:5 (NKJV), *"Hear me Levites! Now sanctify yourselves, sanctify the house of the Lord God of your fathers and carry out the rubbish from the holy place"*

Do you take time to sanctify yourself?
What does this mean to you?

Deliberate Self-Denial

So it was, when I heard these words, that I sat down and wept, and mourned for many days; **I was fasting and praying before the God of heaven.** *And I said: "I pray, LORD God of heaven, O great and awesome God, You who keep Your covenant and mercy with those who love You and observe Your commandments, please let Your ear be attentive and Your eyes open, that You may hear the prayer of Your servant which I pray before You now, day and night...*
(Nehemiah 1:4-6 NKJV).

FASTING is a form of deliberate self-denial. It is a sacrificial form of yielding oneself to deeper things of God's spirituality in your life. It enhances the human spirit while bringing the body and soul to the subjection of Jesus Christ.

A three-day fast is reminiscent of Esther's fast, and it is still as powerful today as it was then. Fasting reduces the influence of your flesh—the carnal nature—and enhances your spirit.

Fasting brings your spirituality up to a new level in God.

Do you fast? What does fasting mean to you?

Fasting,
Continued

*Blow the trumpet in Zion, **declare a holy fast,** call a sacred assembly. Gather the people, consecrate the assembly bring together the elders, gather the children, those nursing at the breast. Let the bridegroom leave his room and the bride her chamber* (Joel 2:15-16).

MAY the Lord have mercy and do something amazing for you and among you.

Don't indulge in self-pity because you are fasting!

***But when you fast,** put oil on your head and wash your face, so that it will not be obvious to others that you are fasting, but only to your Father, who is unseen; and your Father, who sees what is done in secret, will reward you* (Matthew 6:17-19).

Jesus was specific about not using fasting as a form of self-righteousness. Many believers announce their fasting, a direct contradiction to the verse above. The reward from your heavenly Father is all that you need.

Do you know about the several different types of fasting?

Proclaiming and Healing

Jesus went throughout Galilee, teaching in their synagogues, proclaiming the good news of the kingdom, and healing every disease and sickness among the people (Matthew 4:23).

JUST as Jesus did, we are asked to do the same—proclaim the good news of the Kingdom of God.

As a result, people brought the sick into the streets and laid them on beds and mats so that at least Peter's shadow might fall on some of them as he passed by (Acts 5:15).

Just as Peter's shadow healed those suffering from sickness, we are asked to provide healing to those we know are in need of Jesus' touch.

Have you been to a healing service?

A Second Chance

Then God blessed Noah and his sons, saying to them, "Be fruitful and increase in number and fill the earth. The fear and dread of you will fall on all the beasts of the earth, and on all the birds in the sky, on every creature that moves along the ground, and on all the fish in the sea; they are given into your hands. Everything that lives and moves about will be food for you. Just as I gave you the green plants, ***I now give you everything*** (Genesis 9:1-3).

G OD blessed and gave the earth a second chance by rescuing and blessing Noah and his family.

The first man on earth failed and fell short of God's expectations. Humankind fell from the heightened level of God's consciousness and intimacy! But God in His infinite mercy gave humankind a second chance to regain the privileges lost by Adam by the blessings of Noah.

May God bless you with Noah's blessings.

Are you grateful when you are granted a second chance? Do you extend the same mercy to others?

Family Blessings

*Then all the people left, each for their own home, and David
returned home to bless his family* (1 Chronicles 16:43).

W HEN you invite God into your home, your entire family will be
blessed, *"The ark of God remained with the family of Obed-
Edom in his house for three months, and the LORD blessed his household and everything he had"* (1 Chron. 13:14).

Just as David went home to bless his family and the Obed-Edom
family hosted the ark of God, you, too, can bring blessings to your
family as you are obedient to His Word and faithful as His humble
servant.

Have you invited God into your home recently?

Becoming Like Him

*I want to know Christ—yes, to know the power of his resur-
rection and participation in his sufferings, **becoming like
him** in his death, and so, somehow, attaining to the resurrection from the dead* (Philippians 3:10-11).

I pray that you will "know the power of His resurrection" in your
life more than ever before. Who can write as Paul did about his
relationship with Christ? Today's believers are so very fortunate to
have the Holy Bible—and all the different versions—so we can step
back into the time of Christ, and even before, to know Him, to know
the triune God.

*And as John wrote, Beloved, now we are children of God; and
it has not yet been revealed what we shall be, but we know
that when He is revealed, **we shall be like Him**, for we shall
see Him as He is* (1 John 3:2).

How Christ-like have you become since
you became a believer?

To Crucify

Behold, we are going up to Jerusalem, and the Son of Man will be betrayed to the chief priests and to the scribes; and they will condemn Him to death, and deliver Him to the Gentiles to mock and to scourge and to crucify. And the third day He will rise again (Matthew 20:18-20 NKJV).

CHRIST was born and raised in this world so He could fulfill His purpose—redemption of humankind. The suffering he endured during those last days and moments are enough make most believers fall to their knees in humble adoration.

Are you awed by the sacrifice of God by giving up His Son for your redemption?

Beware of Strange Doctrine

Do not be carried away by all kinds of strange teachings. It is good for our hearts to be strengthened by grace, not by eating ceremonial foods, which is of no benefit to those who do so (Hebrews 13:9).

Be not carried about with divers and strange doctrines. For it is a good thing that the heart be established with grace... (Hebrews 13:9 KJV).

THERE are many false teachings and strange doctrines floating around these days. With the ease of worldwide communication, people—and believers as well—are being exposed to a variety of beliefs that are contrary to the Word of God. Some are so similar that it is hard for even seasoned believers to distinguish. It is very important to be discerning—read the Bible and listen for the Holy Spirit's direction.

Are you easily carried away by the latest religious fad or teaching?

The Spirit of Grace

*For you **have not come** to the mountain that may be touched and that burned with fire, and to blackness and darkness and tempest, and the sound of a trumpet and the voice of words, so that those who heard it begged that the word should not be spoken to them anymore. (For they could not endure what was commanded: "And if so much as a beast touches the mountain, it shall be stoned or shot with an arrow." And so terrifying was the sight that Moses said, "I am exceedingly afraid and trembling.") But you **have come** to Mount Zion and to the city of the living God, the heavenly Jerusalem, to an innumerable company of angels, to the general assembly and church of the firstborn who are registered in heaven, to God the Judge of all, to the spirits of just men made perfect, **to Jesus the Mediator of the new covenant,** and to the blood of sprinkling that speaks better things than that of Abel* (Hebrews 12:18-24 NKJV).

Y ou are living in the days of God's grace. His law is no longer judged as harshly as in the Old Testament where, *"Anyone who rejected the law of Moses **died without mercy** on the testimony of two or three witnesses"* (Heb. 10:28).

Because of Jesus, the Son of God, you have the love of a merciful heavenly Father. He is your Mediator—the only Person between you and your Almighty God. There need be no other.

How often do you realize that it is by grace we have been saved,

Mercy Trumps Judgment

Speak and act as those who are going to be judged by the law that gives freedom, because judgment without mercy will be shown to anyone who has not been merciful. Mercy triumphs over judgment (James 2:12-13).

Daily believers need to be mindful of how truly merciful God is. Without His grace and mercy, the world would be a miserable place—more terrible than imaginable.

May you always acknowledge His faithfulness by showing mercy and grace to others—at home, work, church, in the grocery store. His children are to exhibit the traits of Jesus, and He was at all times graceful and merciful. Even when He overturned the tables in the temple, He was showing restraint, for He was more than capable of destroying every person in the place.

Do you regularly show God's mercy through extending mercy to others?

Blessed Are the Merciful

Blessed are the merciful, for they will be shown mercy
(Matthew 5:7).

I believe that it is within all believers to be blessed, as all believers can show mercy. As Matthew wrote, "Blessed are the merciful..." he knew that when a person shows mercy, that same mercy will be returned.

> *We have different gifts, according to **the grace given to each of us.** If your gift is prophesying, then prophesy in accordance with your faith; if it is serving, then serve; if it is teaching, then teach; if it is to encourage, then give encouragement; if it is giving, then give generously; if it is to lead, do it diligently; if it is to **show mercy, do it cheerfully*** (Romans 12:6-9).

Although Paul seems to say that showing mercy is a gift to some, I believe that mercy, as grace, is accorded to us all. There is within us the ability to show mercy cheerfully. May you perfect this gift by sharing it with all those surrounding you. This will make your world a better place—for everyone.

Who is the first person who comes to mind when you think about showing mercy?

Keep Calling His Name

Then they came to Jericho. As Jesus and his disciples, together with a large crowd, were leaving the city, a blind man, Bartimaeus (which means "son of Timaeus"), was sitting by the roadside begging. When he heard that it was Jesus of Nazareth, **he began to shout, "Jesus, Son of David, have mercy on me!"** *Many rebuked him and told him to be quiet, but* **he shouted all the more,** *"Son of David, have mercy on me!" Jesus stopped and said, "Call him." So they called to the blind man, "Cheer up! On your feet! He's calling you." Throwing his cloak aside, he jumped to his feet and came to Jesus* (Mark 10:46-50).

D ON'T allow others to keep you from calling out the name of Jesus. In these troubled times of economic, emotional, and physical distress, many are calling on financial managers, doctors, and psychics to solve their problems.

But only One can truly bring peace in the midst of noisy crowds or the silent agony of an empty bedroom. They told the blind man to "Cheer up! Jesus is calling you!"

Keep calling on Jesus—He will return your call.

**How many times do you call on Jesus
before you give up?**

Reading the Bible in a Year: Daniel 5-6 & 1 John 4.

Failing Eyesight

How can you say to your brother, 'Brother, let me take the speck out of your eye,' when you yourself fail to see the plank in your own eye? You hypocrite, first take the plank out of your eye, and then you will see clearly to remove the speck from your brother's eye (Luke 6:42).

HAVE you ever told someone what to do or spoken harshly about someone, and then later found out that your assumptions were entirely unfounded? Luke was telling us that we need to examine ourselves before we start telling others what to do.

Many in these times consider themselves "control freaks" and are sure that they know best for themselves and others. Others are so focused on others that they don't see the flaws in their own selves.

May you live in the balanced perspective of considering your own biases and perspectives before pointing them out in others.

Do you see your failings before those of others?

Allow Him to Wash Your Feet

After that, he poured water into a basin and began to wash his disciples' feet, drying them with the towel that was wrapped around him. He came to Simon Peter, who said to him, "Lord, are you going to wash my feet?" Jesus replied, "You do not realize now what I am doing, but later you will understand." "No," said Peter, "you shall never wash my feet." **Jesus answered, "Unless I wash you, you have no part with me."** *"Then, Lord," Simon Peter replied, "not just my feet but my hands and my head as well!" Jesus answered, "Those who have had a bath need only to wash their feet; their whole body is clean...* (John 13:5-10).

PETER couldn't understand that Jesus came to the world as a Servant—One who was committed to serving God's children. While washing someone's feet is a very humbling experience, Jesus was not ashamed; He was not above such a lowly task.

We know how Peter reacted; how do you think the others felt as they watched their Master kneel before them and pour water over their dirty feet and then dry them with the towel.

Will you allow Jesus to wash your feet?

Show and Tell Christian

However, I consider my life worth nothing to me; my only aim is to finish the race and complete the task the Lord Jesus has given me—the task of testifying to the good news of God's grace (Acts 20:24).

Paul was a show and tell apostle. He didn't just sit in his home and think about telling others about God's grace. No. He traveled his known world to testify the good news to all who would listen.

All the things he accomplished before he became a believer didn't matter anymore. All of the goals he achieved, all of the honors he received were "worth nothing" to him. His only aim was to finish the race and complete the task of sharing the gospel with as many people as possible.

Will you continue to testify to the good news?

Are You Convinced?

For I am convinced that neither death nor life, neither angels nor demons, neither the present nor the future, nor any powers, neither height nor depth, nor anything else in all creation, will be able to separate us from the love of God that is in Christ Jesus our Lord (Romans 8:38-39).

P AUL was convinced that nothing could separate him—or anyone who believes in Jesus Christ as the Son of God—from the love of God. What a reassuring passage of Scripture.

There is nothing else in this world that you can be absolutely sure of as the promise made in Romans. People will let you down; your career could slip away; your finances can vanish; your friends betray you—but there is nothing that will ever separate you from the love of your heavenly Father.

Does this Scripture bring peace to your heart?

Love Sweet Love

Love is patient, love is kind. It does not envy, it does not boast, it is not proud. It does not dishonor others, it is not self-seeking, it is not easily angered, it keeps no record of wrongs. Love does not delight in evil but rejoices with the truth. It always protects, always trusts, always hopes, always perseveres. Love never fails. But where there are prophecies, they will cease; where there are tongues, they will be stilled; where there is knowledge, it will pass away. For we know in part and we prophesy in part, but when completeness comes, what is in part disappears. When I was a child, I talked like a child, I thought like a child, I reasoned like a child. When I became a man, I put the ways of childhood behind me. For now we see only a reflection as in a mirror; then we shall see face to face. Now I know in part; then I shall know fully, even as I am fully known. And now these three remain: faith, hope and love.
But the greatest of these is love (1 Corinthians 13:4-13).

How can you ever aspire to love like that? Only by the grace of God can you stop being envious, boastful, and proud. Only with the Holy Spirit living in you can you forget wrongs, stop dwelling on evil, and rejoice in the truth. Only through the love of Jesus can we trust a future that we only know in part. And only when we have faith, hope, and love will we fully be alive.

Are you ready to share His love with others today?

Not Crushed

*But we have this treasure in jars of clay to show that this all-surpassing **power is from God** and not from us. We are hard pressed on every side, but not crushed; perplexed, but not in despair; persecuted, but not abandoned; struck down, but not destroyed* (2 Corinthians 4:7-9).

You may be facing terrible circumstances. Maybe your home is being repossessed, your child is ill, your parents need more help than you can give—no matter what is challenging you today, God's Word says that you will not be crushed, you will not be in despair, you will not be abandoned or destroyed.

God promises that His power will sustain you. May you feel His power today throughout each and every circumstance. May His love overwhelm you.

Can you give your problem to God and know that He will solve it for you?

Love Your Neighbor

*You, my brothers and sisters, were called to be free. But do
not use your freedom to indulge the flesh; rather, serve one
another humbly in love. For the entire law is fulfilled in
keeping this one command: "Love your neighbor as yourself"*
(Galatians 5:13-14).

THIS command is hard for many people, including believers, to
keep. Physical neighbors as well as spiritual neighbors can be
hard to get along with at times. Maybe they don't mow their grass,
maybe they don't pray as often as you think they should. There are
many fleshly reasons not to love your neighbor.

But the "as yourself" part is even harder to keep. We are so critical of ourselves and the world so condemning if we don't look, talk,
act in society's accepted way.

May you come to love yourself as God loves you—then you will
easily follow through with His command to love your neighbor.

**How hard is it for you to love yourself?
Your neighbor?**

As God Forgave You

Get rid of all bitterness, rage and anger, brawling and slander, along with every form of malice. Be kind and compassionate to one another, forgiving each other, just as in Christ God forgave you (Ephesians 4:31-32).

GOD forgives you through Christ. Christ forgives you through His endless love for you. For His sake you are kind and compassionate to others—even when you don't want to or you think they don't deserve your kindness.

We can't be like those who don't believe—those who are bitter, angry, and cause all types of troubles for others, those who don't know His forgiveness.

Your focus, like that of Jesus, must be on spreading His love to all who will listen. For all have sinned and need to know that they are forgiven by the One who died to redeem them.

How forgiving are you?

His Holy Name

*Therefore God exalted him [Jesus] to the highest place
and gave him the name that is above every name, that at
the name of Jesus every knee should bow, in heaven and
on earth and under the earth, and every tongue acknowledge that Jesus Christ is Lord, to the glory of God the Father*
(Philippians 2:9-11).

THE name of Jesus makes a people react. Whether they react with
goodness or badness depends on their relationship with the One
who loves them unconditionally.

You have heard the name of Jesus and God Almighty used as a
curse word—taken in vain. This ought not to be. Rather, at the sound
of His name, every knee should bow and every tongue confess that
Jesus Christ is Lord!

**How can you exalt His name today
in a special way?**

With the Lord Forever

*For the Lord himself will come down from heaven, with a loud command, with the voice of the archangel and with the trumpet call of God, and the dead in Christ will rise first. After that, we who are still alive and are left will be caught up together with them in the clouds to meet the Lord in the air. And so **we will be with the Lord forever.** Therefore encourage one another with these words* (1 Thessalonians 4:16-18).

As you anticipate that glorious day when the Lord returns, are you enjoying His presence even now? Many are so focused on the hereafter, they are not pursuing their full potential here on earth—as God intended.

God delights when His children are about His business during their earthly lifetimes. He placed each person in a specific time and location so that His will would be accomplished. May you seek His face not only in the clouds on that day but every day in all of your movements.

Are you living in the will of God for your life?

True Success

*But godliness with contentment is great gain. For we brought
nothing into the world, and we can take nothing out of it. But
if we have food and clothing, we will be content with that.
Those who want to get rich fall into temptation and a trap
and into many foolish and harmful desires that plunge people into ruin and destruction* (1 Timothy 6:6-9).

GODLINESS with contentment is true success. Godliness is a genuine day-by-day walk with God. Contentment is choosing to be
satisfied.

In this modern age where instant satisfaction is expected and
being rich is the goal of many, the rate of suicide and the number of
people taking legal and illegal drugs is rising.

Learning how to be content with what you have is the secret
of living an enjoyable life filled with peace and love. True success,
indeed!

How successful are you?

A Mist

*Why, you do not even know what will happen tomorrow. What is your life? You are a mist that appears for a little while and then vanishes. Instead, you ought to say, **"If it is the Lord's will, we will live and do this or that."** As it is, you boast in your arrogant schemes. All such boasting is evil* (James 4:14-16).

IT is true that your life is but a short expanse of time when considering eternity, but you must make this time count for Christ.

As many make boasts about this and that, believers need to be following God's will, actively seeking His direction for their lives. Tomorrow is not promised to anyone—only God knows the number of your days.

But knowing for absolutely sure that He has your best interests in His heart of hearts, you can sleep soundly each night knowing that if tomorrow does arrive, it should be lived to His glory.

**Every morning, do you consider
God's will for your life?**

Repay Evil with Blessing

*Finally, all of you, **be like-minded, be sympathetic, love one another, be compassionate and humble.** Do not repay evil with evil or insult with insult. On the contrary, **repay evil with blessing,** because to this you were called so that you may inherit a blessing. For, "Whoever would love life and see good days must keep their tongue from evil and their lips from deceitful speech. They must turn from evil and do good; they must seek peace and pursue it. For the eyes of the Lord are on the righteous and his ears are attentive to their prayer, but the face of the Lord is against those who do evil"* (1 Peter 3:8-12).

THERE is much good advice in this passage in First Peter. If taken seriously, you will live a life full of blessings galore! Not repaying evil for evil is contrary to the Old Testament's eye for an eye. Jesus turned the page of retribution and revenge.

Do not repay evil with evil; be sympathetic, love one another, don't speak evil, and don't be deceitful. If you do good, seek peace, and pray, the Lord will hear your prayer and you will inherit a blessing.

May you commit today to obeying these ways of the Lord.

Are you one prone to taking revenge rather than allowing God to serve justice?

In His Time

But do not forget this one thing, dear friends: With the Lord a day is like a thousand years, and a thousand years are like a day. The Lord is not slow in keeping his promise, as some understand slowness. Instead he is patient with you, not wanting anyone to perish, but everyone to come to repentance (2 Peter 3:8-9).

GOD's timing is not your timing. Only He is aware of all things—past, present, and future—and only He knows what will best affect lives, cities, nations at certain times.

God always keeps His promises—He is not too slow or too fast. His timing is perfect. He is patient about His second coming because He wants everyone to come to repentance.

Have you been waiting on Him to make a decision about your career, your family, your finances? Have you been waiting for Him to return in all of His glory? In His perfect timing, all things will be decided and He will return. Trust and have faith.

Do you base His timing on a day or a thousand years?

Greater Is He

*You, dear children, are from God and have overcome them, because **the one who is in you is greater** than the one who is in the world* (1 John 4:4).

ALWAYS remember that God in you is greater than the evil that is in the world. Nothing can topple you when you are standing with the Lord. The Holy Spirit anchors you to the Word of God, and armed with that sharp sword, you can destroy every obstacle.

When others turn to drugs, sex, fame, or wealth as comfort and for security, they substitute the inner peace of God's presence with evil. When tempted by these temporal things, may your spirit be quickened and your mind reminded of First John 4:4.

Who is living in you?

Glory and Honor and Power

You are worthy, our Lord and God, to receive glory and honor and power, for you created all things, and by your will they were created and have their being (Revelation 4:11).

Our God has all the glory and honor and power throughout eternity. As His children we are to recognize this and respectfully fear Him. He created us to love us; not even a sparrow dies without Him knowing about it.

Bringing His reality into your daily life partners you with the King of kings; you will be empowered to become the best person possible each day. He will give you the words to say, the plan that will work, the love that will last.

I pray that you will avail yourself of all He desires to give you— every day in every way.

Is your heart, mind, and spirit open
to receive His partnership?

Worthy

In a loud voice they [angels] *were saying: "Worthy is the Lamb, who was slain, to receive power and wealth and wisdom and strength and honor and glory and praise!" Then I heard every creature in heaven and on earth and under the earth and on the sea, and all that is in them, saying: "To him who sits on the throne and to the Lamb be praise and honor and glory and power, for ever and ever!"* (Revelation 5:12-13).

JESUS was the Lamb who was slain—for you. How can we ever repay Him for what He did for humanity?

We can obey His commands; we can love each other; we can bring others to the saving knowledge of His redemptive power.

May you always consider Him worthy of your praise and worship. Through Jesus Christ, may your prayers be constant in admiration and thanksgiving to the One true God.

How worthy are you of Jesus' sacrifice?

A New Heaven and New Earth

Then I saw "a new heaven and a new earth," for the first heaven and the first earth had passed away, and there was no longer any sea. I saw the Holy City, the new Jerusalem, coming down out of heaven from God, prepared as a bride beautifully dressed for her husband (Revelation 21:1-2).

BRIDES are beautiful—they take special care to have the right dress, the perfect hairdo, their bodies are washed and their nails are manicured. The new Jerusalem will be perfectly adorned to be placed within the new heaven and new earth.

John shares in the Book of Revelation many visions and we may not understand all of what he saw, but we can be assured that God knows what He is doing. He knows when the time is right, and He knows where you will be when it happens.

Trust in God from Genesis through Revelation. He will never leave you or forsake you—on this you can depend.

**Are you ready for whatever God has
in store for the world?**

No More Tears

He [God] *will wipe every tear from their eyes. There will be no more death or mourning or crying or pain, for the old order of things has passed away. He who was seated on the throne said, "I am making everything new!" Then he said, "Write this down, for these words are trustworthy and true." He said to me* [John]: *"It is done. I am the Alpha and the Omega, the Beginning and the End. To the thirsty I will give water without cost from the spring of the water of life. Those who are victorious will inherit all this, and I will be their God and they will be my children* (Revelation 21:4-7).

WHAT a glorious time that will be! Imagine a world where no one has reason to cry. Where pain and death are no more. Those who believe are eternally victorious and they will drink from the spring of the water of life.

You will be with God forevermore—all that this life has caused you to fear, loath, and grieve over will not even be a memory. Your entire being will have passed away and only joy and His splendid light will be before you.

Can you imagine this kind of world?

Behold a Sign

*Therefore the Lord himself will give you a sign: The virgin will
conceive and give birth to a son, and will call him Immanuel.
He will be eating curds and honey when he knows enough to
reject the wrong and choose the right* (Isaiah 7:14-15).

IMMANUEL—GOD with you. Because Jesus is with us always and He
knows enough to reject the wrong and choose the right, we too
should know enough. We can decide the right way to go, people to
befriend, career to pursue, decisions to make.

With divine guidance from the Holy Spirit, there is no doubt that
you can make the right choices throughout your life. As you lean
on His understanding of each situation—not your own—you can be
assured of staying on the path toward God's destiny for you.

Be aware of the signs He gives you.

How cognizant are you of His signs?

Do Not be Afraid

*The angel went to her and said, "Greetings, you who are highly favored! The Lord is with you." Mary was greatly troubled at his words and wondered what kind of greeting this might be. But the angel said to her, "**Do not be afraid,** Mary; you have found favor with God. You will conceive and give birth to a son, and you are to call him Jesus. He will be great and will be called the Son of the Most High. The Lord God will give him the throne of his father David, and he will reign over Jacob's descendants forever; his kingdom will never end"* (Luke 1:28-33).

Too many times, rather than seek understanding, we first allow fear to stun us. Moving past the initial response is critical. Mary was comforted by the angel's command and then stunned again with what the angel told her. Although she was confronted with an amazing and unbelievable proclamation, she accepted it—no doubt because the Lord's favor prepared her.

Living a righteous life will bring with it the Lord's favor. May your life reflect His righteousness and favor.

Are you afraid of things you don't understand?

An Angel Appeared

*And there were shepherds living out in the fields nearby, keeping watch over their flocks at night. An angel of the Lord appeared to them, and the glory of the Lord shone around them, and they were terrified. But the angel said to them, "Do not be afraid. I bring you good news that will cause **great joy for all the people** (Luke 2:8-10).*

A GAIN an angel appeared, and this time the shepherds were afraid—even terrified! But the angel told them not to be afraid. This angel was bringing them "good news that will cause great joy for all the people."

All the people. Not just the shepherds, not just the parents and relatives of the baby—*all* people. This "great joy" continues to be experienced, centuries after the birth, by people worldwide.

Sometimes it is easy for Christians to think they are the only ones who need to hear the Word, feel God's touch, and learn about His ways. Not so. Jesus became flesh and blood so *all* people would experience great joy.

**How willing are you to share the joy of Christmas
with people of other faiths?**

Born to You This Day

For there is born to you this day in the city of David a Savior, who is Christ the Lord. And this will be the sign to you: You will find a Babe wrapped in swaddling cloths, lying in a manger." And suddenly there was with the angel a multitude of the heavenly host praising God and saying: "Glory to God in the highest, and on earth peace, goodwill toward men!"
(Luke 2:11-14 NKJV).

THIS day was unlike any other day. The babe born this day that the angel told the shepherds about would change the world. His influence would permeate the towns and cities around Bethlehem and then spread worldwide.

The name of Jesus continues to bring hope—and horror—to millions of people. This baby who was wrapped in blankets and placed in a feed trough introduced a new era of God's reign in the world. His presence would be felt by everyone who came in contact with Him— and continues to affect all those who hear His Word.

**Will you join the heavenly host and
praise Him before others?**

Your Salvation

Moved by the Spirit, he [Simeon] *went into the temple courts. When the parents brought in the child Jesus to do for him what the custom of the Law required, Simeon took him in his arms and praised God, saying: "Sovereign Lord, as you have promised, you may now dismiss your servant in peace. For **my eyes have seen your salvation, which you have prepared in the sight of all nations:** a light for revelation to the Gentiles, and the glory of your people Israel* (Luke 2:27-32).

JESUS is the light of the entire world—the salvation of all nations. Simeon knew by the Spirit of the Lord that he had seen God's Son. This is the Son God sent to the world so that none would perish, His only begotten Son that whoever would believe in Him would have eternal life (see John 3:16).

On that first Christmas, the day of Jesus' birth, only God knew for sure what an impact He would have on creation. Thanks to the faithful used by the Holy Spirit, the Bible tells the story. Now it is up to us to share that story with others.

Have your eyes seen your salvation through the pages of God's Word?

Counterfeit Spirits at Christmas

Then Simeon blessed them and said to Mary, his mother: "This child is destined to cause the falling and rising of many in Israel, and to be a sign that will be spoken against, so that the thoughts of many hearts will be revealed. And a sword will pierce your own soul too (Luke 2:34-35).

CHRISTMAS is as much a time for festivities as it is for prayers. Many in today's world have taken the festivities far above the reason for the season. There is an ever-increasing need for prayerfulness in a world that is evil and where idolatrous worship is celebrated.

There is an increase in activities of satanic groups, especially during the Christmas season. This is the time, therefore, for both festivities and intensified prayers.

Blessings of the Lord be upon you today and all that is yours. May the Prince of Peace truly be with you always as you covenant with Jesus Christ.

Do you celebrate Christ each Christmas— and throughout the year?

True Christmas

Coming up to them at that very moment, she gave thanks to God and spoke about the child to all who were looking forward to the redemption of Jerusalem. When Joseph and Mary had done everything required by the Law of the Lord, they returned to Galilee to their own town of Nazareth. **And the child grew and became strong; he was filled with wisdom, and the grace of God was on him** (Luke 2:38-40).

CHRISTMAS is all about Jesus Christ.

Yes indeed, it is the celebration of Jesus' earthly birthday. Despite the commercialization, despite the politics, His birth will always remain the eternal truth.

A joy that is universal; think of it—everyone, no matter who you are, big or small, poor or rich, male or female, black or white, Jew or Gentile. Joy is the true spirit of Christmas. It is about the birth of Jesus; have Christmas dinner together and plenty of attention for the children, but Christ must be the center of Christmas.

The true message of Christmas is about the dawn of the bright Light for those in darkness, hope in the midst of despair! There is hope, no matter the situation or the challenges that may confront you.

Are your Christmas celebrations centered on the birth of Christ?

CONTACT INFORMATION

For additional copies of this book and other products from Cross House Books, contact: sales@crosshousebooks.co.uk.

Please visit our Website for product updates and news at www.crosshousebooks.co.uk.

OTHER INQUIRIES

CROSS HOUSE BOOKS
Christian Book Publishers
245 Midstocket Road, Aberdeen, AB15 5PH, UK

info@crosshousebooks.co.uk
publisher@crosshousebooks.co.uk

"The entrance of Your Word brings light."

DO YOU WANT TO BECOME
A PUBLISHED AUTHOR
AND GET YOUR BOOK DISTRIBUTED
WORLDWIDE BY MAJOR BOOK STORES?

Contact:
admin@crosshousebooks.co.uk
www.crosshousebooks.co.uk.
or write to
CROSS HOUSE BOOKS
245 Midstocket Road, Aberdeen, AB15 5PH, UK

MINISTRY INFORMATION

Dr. Joe Ibojie is the Senior Pastor of
THE FATHER'S HOUSE

The Father's House is a family church and a vibrant community of Christians located in Aberdeen, Scotland, UK. The Father's House seeks to build a bridge of hope across generations, racial divides, and gender biases through the ministry of the Word.

You are invited to come and worship if you are in the area.

For location, please visit the church's Website:
www.the-fathers-house.org.uk

For inquiries:
info@the-fathers-house.org.uk
Call 44 1224 701343

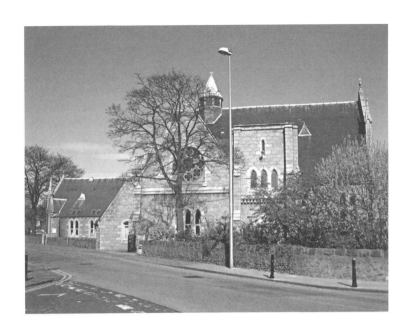

New Home of The Father's House Located at
Caroline Place, Aberdeen AB25 2TH

NEW TITLES FROM
CROSS HOUSE BOOKS

40 Names of the Holy Spirit

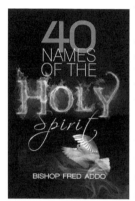

The names of God represent a deliberate *invitation to you* to take advantage of what God can and wants to be in your life. Whatever you call Him is what He will become to you. Do you know all of His names? How much deeper would you like to know the Comforter?

You will learn the following—and much more!

- Seven Symbols of the Holy Spirit
- Names of the Holy Spirit
- Seven Things *Not* to Do to the Holy Spirit
- Twentyfold Relationship with the Holy Spirit
- Fourfold Presence of the Holy Spirit
- Seven Keys to Receiving the Holy Spirit Baptism

Each chapter concludes with Points to Ponder designed to stimulate and inspire you to reach a higher level of spiritual knowledge and living. The Holy Spirit is your Strengthener—learn how to enlist His personal help today!

Destined for the Top

Destined for the Top presents simple and proven successful answers to life's most complex questions. Divided into two parts—Life Issues and Family Issues—you can be at the top of your game in every aspect of your life by knowing what and who to avoid during your journey to the top.

Through an added feature of thought-provoking questions at the end of each chapter, you will learn how to strengthen your spirit, invest in your potential, and realize how fickle your feelings really are. You will discover how worldly ambition prohibits your advancement and how God's wisdom and love through you propels you toward fulfilling your destiny!

BOOKS BY DR. JOE IBOJIE

How to Live the Supernatural Life in the Here and Now—BEST SELLER

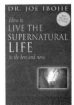

Are you ready to stop living an ordinary life? You were meant to live a supernatural life! God intends us to experience His power every day! In *How to Live the Supernatural Life in the Here and Now* you will learn how to bring the supernatural power of God into everyday living. Finding the proper balance for your life allows you to step into the supernatural and to move in power and authority over everything around you. Dr. Joe Ibojie, an experienced pastor and prolific writer, provides practical steps and instruction that will help you to:

- Step out of the things that hold you back in life.
- Understand that all life is spiritual.
- Experience the supernatural life that God has planned for you!
- Find balance between the natural and the spiritual.
- Release God's power to change and empower your circumstances.

Are you ready to live a life of spiritual harmony? Then you are ready to learn *How to Live the Supernatural Life in the Here and Now!*

Dreams and Visions Volume 1—BEST SELLER

Dreams and Visions presents sound scriptural principles and practical instructions to help you understand dreams and visions. The book provides readers with the necessary understanding to approach dreams and visions by the Holy Spirit through biblical illustrations, understanding of the meaning of dreams and prophetic symbolism, and by exploring the art of dream interpretation according to ancient methods of the Bible.

Dreams and Visions Volume 2—NEW

God speaks to you through dreams and visions. Do you want to know the meaning of your dreams? Do you want to know what He is telling and showing you? Now you can know!

Dreams and Visions Volume 2 is packed full of exciting and Bible-guided ways to discover the meaning of your God-inspired, dreamy nighttime adventures and your wide-awake supernatural experiences!

Dr. Joe Ibojie reveals why and how God wants to communicate with you through dreams and visions. In this *second volume,* the teaching emphasizes how to gain clearer understanding of your dreams and visions in a new, in-depth, and user-friendly way.

Illustrated Bible-Based Dictionary of Dream Symbols—BEST SELLER

Illustrated Bible-Based Dictionary of Dream Symbols is much more than a book of dream symbols. This book is a treasure chest, loaded down with revelation and the hidden mysteries of God that have been waiting since before the foundation of the earth to be uncovered. Whether you use this book to assist in interpreting your dreams or as an additional resource for your study of the Word of God, you will find it a welcome companion.

EXPANDED AND ENRICHED
WITH EXCITING NEW CONTENT

Bible-Based Dictionary of Prophetic Symbols for Every Christian—NEW

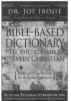

The most comprehensive, illustrated Bible-based dictionary of prophetic and dream symbols ever compiled is contained in this one authoritative book!

The Bible-Based Dictionary of Prophetic Symbols for Every Christian is a masterpiece that intelligently and understandably bridges the gap between prophetic revelation and application—PLUS it includes the expanded version of the best selling *Illustrated Bible-Based Dictionary of Dream Symbols.*

Expertly designed, researched, and Holy Spirit inspired to provide you an extensive wealth of revelation knowledge about symbols and symbolic actions, this book is divided into four parts that go way beyond listing and defining words. Rhema word and divine prompting lift off every page!

The Justice of God: Victory in Everyday Living—NEW

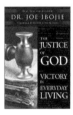

Only once in awhile does a book bring rare insight and godly illumination to a globally crucial subject. This book is one of them! A seminal work from a true practitioner, best-selling author, and leader of a vibrant church, Dr. Joe Ibojie brings clarity and a hands-on perspective to the Justice of God.

The Justice of God reveals:

- How to pull down your blessings.
- How to regain your inheritance.
- The heavenly courts of God.
- How to work with angels.
- The power and dangers of prophetic acts and drama.

The Watchman: The Ministry of the Seer in the Local Church—NEW

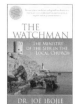

The ministry of the watchman in a local church is possibly one of the most common and yet one of the most misunderstood ministries in the Body of Christ. Over time, the majority of these gifted people have been driven into reclusive lives because of relational issues and confusion surrounding their very vital ministry in the local church.

Through the pages of *The Watchman* you will learn:

- Who these watchmen are.
- How they can be recognized, trained, appreciated, and integrated into the Body of Christ.
- About their potential and how they can be channelled as valuable resources to the local leadership.
- How to avoid prophetic and pastoral pitfalls.
- How to receive these gifted folks as the oracles of God they really are.

The 21st century watchman ministry needs a broader and clearer definition. It is time that the conservative, narrow, and restrictive perspectives of the watchman's ministry be enlarged into the reality of its great potential and value God has intended.

Korean translations:
Dreams and Visions Volume 1

Italian translation:
Dreams and Visions Volume 1

The Final Frontiers—Countdown to the Final Showdown

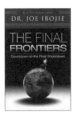

The Final Frontiers—Countdown to the Final Showdown peers profoundly into the future. It expertly explores the emerging cosmic involvement of the seemingly docile elements of nature and their potential to completely alter the ways of warfare.

In preparation for this impending battle, Christians need to understand the dynamics of their authority and spiritual domain of influence. The power of proclamation and the elemental forces of nature—ground, sun, ancient mountains, moon, and the deep water beneath—are divine weapons in God's arsenal.

Christians must not allow the things that are supposed to bless them to become instruments of judgment or punishment. *The Final Frontiers* provides you with a practical approach to the changing struggles that confront humanity now and in your future.

The Final Frontiers reveals through Scriptures and modern-day experiences:

- What was lost at the Fall
- Invisible realms of hell
- The elements of nature in God's service
- Spiritual weaponry
- How to defeat the devil at the mind game
- Peace and the ultimate redemption

The earth can either rise up against humankind, or it can be subdued in the service of God. *The choice is yours.*